The Life and Times

Written and illustrated by Bill Bradley.
Alias Bandy Bill.

I thought about it ten years ago. I started it about five years ago, I got serious about it twelve months ago. I registered it with two hours to go Bill Bradley alias Bandy Bill 2015 HPO 2292015

At this stage I would like to thank John Hoyle, Pat Bluhm, Derron Gilhooly and my two granddaughters Suzanne and Jenny Dalziel for all their help and patience they have shown me whilst putting this work together

Thank you all

Forward

When people say to me "I believe you've written a book," I reply, "No." I've put together a group of photos with and explanation of why they exist. It's about a group of kids, born in the late 1930s, growing up in a free environment in and around Pound Road, Little Sutton, Wirral Cheshire, which is part of Ellesmere Port Urban District Council. Now seventy years on and beyond, we hope we are still pals today.
This was before motorways, M.O.T,S, Health and Safety Laws and written risk assessments.
When being watched by CCTV was a horror science fiction film called, (Big Brother is watching you)
When you were told the risk by other older kids, who in the main, would keep you safe.
When common sense ruled and you accepted the consequences for your actions.
When First Aid meant knowing that if you were stung by a nettle you rubbed it with a dock leaf, or if you were stung by a Wasp, you dabbed it with dolly blue.
When you played Doctor and Nurses, but you never worked for the N.H.S
When the good cowboys always beat the baddies and the Mounties always got their man.

These were fantastic days in all.
Now us younger kids are , in the main, trying to keep the older ones safe.
I hope it will bring a smile to your face, or maybe, a tear to your eye.
I have not researched anything, I've written it as I remember it.
Others may remember it differently. I hope I Haven't offended anyone, but it's as true as I remembered it.

Bill Bradley alias Bandy Bill

Contents

The Big Move

It was about 1941, when I stood in Livingstone Road, Ellesmere Port Cheshire, watching the white vapour streams in the sky, as two aeroplanes fought overhead, when suddenly a man ran up the road shouting, "Get inside, Get inside." Me, my sister Jean, and Henry Reyrolds were quickly bundled under the stairs of the house, and told to stay there, as there was a dog fight going on. A so-called dog fight in those days, was when two aircraft went into battle against each other, in this case, it was a British Spitfire against a German fighter plane. We were told later the Spitty had won and the Jerry had crashed into the River Mersey. I believe the pilot's body was recovered and buried in St Paul's Church, Hooton. I would have been three years old then, as I was born in February 1938, one of five kids, later to become six. There was Me, Jean, Doug, Barb and our Joyce was the eldest. Mum was Girt and Dad was Syd.

Dad Syd Bradley   Mum Gert Bradley

Mum worked at the Bowater Paper Mills and Dad was a very highly skilled gas welder. At the time, we were living in Livingstone Road near to the Reynolds family, whilst we waited for our new R.O,F. House to be built in Little Sutton. The R.O.F. {The Royal Ordinance Factory} at Hooton, known as the 'Rofton', due to it's locality, (R.O.F. Hooton.) is where mum and dad would work making munitions for the war effort. One day, whilst playing in the road, I saw two coalmen with a horse and cart. Being nosy, I ran to see what was happening. The man holding the horse was covered in coal dust and dressed in a leather shoulder harness. The second man, similarly dressed, walked towards me, his white teeth shining against his coal black face. He leaned forward saying, "Have you seen this trick?" as his face came close to mine, his top teeth fell to his bottom lip and started to rattle. It frightened me to death.
I ran into the house screaming and luckily I saw dad

leaning over the kitchen sink, looking into a mirror. Wrapping my arms around his legs, I screamed "The Man The Man." Then to my horror, dad turned round wearing the biggest set of false teeth I have ever seen in my life and said. "What's wrong son?" I threw myself onto the floor shaking from top to bottom, Dad took out the teeth and never wore them again in his life. He passed away in 1978

Sometime later, I found myself sitting in a wooden chair on top of a pile of furniture, on the very same horse and cart, which the coal had been on, but this time we were on our way to our new house in Little Sutton. This was a flat roofed three bed roomed house, with it's own built in air raid shelter. The brand-new estate became known as the Unit, because the Unit Construction Company had built it. It consisted of Station Green Station Avenue, Clayhill Green, Sheepfield Close and Pound Road in which we lived. Being the very end house, number 55, it backed onto a field that formed part of a forty acre small-holding. The side garden was against a small wooded area of about twenty oak trees. As you walked in the back door there was a large pantry, then the hall to the front door, on the right was the kitchen, which had a cast-iron enamelled fuel burner with a copper tank on top.

I say fuel burner, because it burnt anything from coal to potato peelings and on numerous occasions the copper tank would rumble. This was the signal to run the hot water tap to cool it down. At the end of the hall was the shelter, and as you opened the door, there was an 18" inch thick blast wall, which you had to walk round. The room was always dark, due to only having two small windows with outside shutters in case of air raids. In contrast, the front room was a large room with an open fireplace and a bay window. The stairs were concrete leading to three bedrooms and a bathroom. Although I was under school age, I remember going with our Jean to John Street Junior School and being looked after by the headmistress, a little grey-haired lady, Miss Hare, but later started school proper in the back room of the Travellers Rest pub in Ledsham Road, Little Sutton.

It was 1943, when I was dragged kicking and squealing into that room, I remember the teacher, a Miss Crab, a rather large lady in a black dress, black laced up ankle boots, fuzzy hair and a hint of a moustache. While being introduced to her, I spotted the girl who lived next door to me, Judy Rowland. She was siting at a double flapped topped desk, a quiet girl with long blond hair, so I thought

The shelter window (note the hinges for the shutters)

my three mates outside 55 Pound Road Ray Bill and Johnny

it would be a good idea to join her, not noticing Mum had left.

After a short time a strange smell drifted into the room from outside. "Okay boys and girls" said Miss Crab. "All out to play in the orchard and let the men do their work." As we ran out we were nearly bowled over by large beer barrels, being rolled in by draymen, but my aim was to get to the orchard and I did this by following two other lads, who were to become life long friends, Johnny Reed and Ray Gadsby. Johnny lived in the middle sandstone cottage on the Rock Mount on Chester Road, but later moved to No six Pound Road just down from Ray, who lived at No 24. After the war Johnny's Dad had a horse and cart, from which he sold vegetables and fresh fish, direct to the houses in Little Sutton. I followed the two lads up a very steep grassy hill, where we gathered at the top, round a big steel plate. "What's this I asked?" "It's our submarine," Johnny replied lifting the lid. "Do you want to go in?" "no thanks," I said, stepping back. Just then, we were joined by another lad, Steve Sharps, "I'll go in," he said and climbed down a steel ladder, which was attached to the side of a brick shaft. Down he went, shouting, "Dive, Dive, Dive," Following his orders we closed the lid and started to run around, arms outstretched, shooting down the Luftwaffe in our fantasy Spitfires, only to be grabbed by Miss Crab, saying, "All inside children." In front of the class, was a big blackboard and easel, which Miss Crab used when teaching us to read or write, but on this occasion, she used it as a shield.

Bowaters Tower is all that's left
of the paper mill

my old school with Miss Crab
the back room of the pub

"Right, rest time," she called. "Fold your arms on the desk put your head in your arms and close your eyes." Everything went quiet, but I couldn't sleep. So slowly lifting my head, I could see Miss Crab's feet, behind the easel and great puffs of smoke gathering round the blackboard, followed by, a cough and a clearing of the throat. I dropped my head just in time, as she said. "Okay Class, rest time over, all outside to play." Clambering out of the desks, we dashed into the orchard, arms outstretched to take up where we had left off. Giving up looking for the Luftwaffe, we decided it was safe to open the lid of our submarine. Out came "Captain" Steve, none the worse for wear after spending about an hour and a half locked in there Saying. "I would rather be in the air force with you lads and not a submariner on my own." Now fifty and more years on when our paths cross, after the niceties of "How's the wife and kids,?" we always end up laughing about the day we locked Steve in the Anderson air-raid shelter, (or our submarine as we knew it.) in the orchard behind our local pub. The Main school was in Berwick Road and consisted of four class rooms and a big hall, which had sliding doors that divided it into two. The Boy's and Girl's toilets were outside in the playground and had solid wooden seats. You sat over a hole and the water flowed under you constantly, so you got a whiff of any one up stream as their contribution passed under you.

Berwick Road School

There was a small garden where we grew vegetables until they built the concrete school canteen on it. Mr Hughes, was the Headmaster and lived in the school house on the corner of Berwick Road and Chester Road. We also utilised the Scout hut in Heath Lane for music lessons. I remember once being picked for the band and being given the triangle to play, but every time it was my turn to ding once, I would ding twice, so I was drummed out so to speak. My favourite destination was the Presbyterian Church Hall, where we were given free school meals, which included the best rice pudding ever. The hall was situated just up the road from the Presbyterian Church, where you had to attend if you wanted to be in the B.B. "Boys Brigade." This enabled you to pass tests and end up with badges and a uniform.

The Farm

By this time we had settled into our new surroundings in Little Sutton and were very happy there. However one day at home, I heard our Dougy telling Mum he was going to the farm and she asked if he would take me. "I can't," he replied, but it was too late, the seed had been set in my head, I was going to the farm. I followed him over the garden fence and across the field, only to be pushed back and threatened with death, but I kept going until the Boss, Mr Dan Dodd, saw us and said, "Bring him In, I'll look after him." Mr Dodd was a round red faced, fair haired Gentleman, with soft white hands, through constantly washing them between milking each of fourteen cows by hand. He had two sons at war, Wilf and Collin, a daughter Margaret in the tree section of the Land army, known as The Lumber Jill's. Harold, who I never met, a daughter Eva and young Danny, who helped run the farm.

I took to the farm like a duck to water and had no fear of the animals, which compared to me were enormous. We

Young Danny Dodd

had fourteen cows, Billy the Bull, two breeding sows, a dozen hens, eight ducks, Paddy a collie dog, Bruce the Alsatian and two Shire Horses called Jewel and Fashion, later to get a third called Flower.

I don't recall what I did on the farm at the time, but remember standing at the top of Pound Road, looking up to see the sky full of two and four propellered bombers, pulling wide winged gliders and the ground vibrating

Flower looking over Gibbons gate

Old Cavalry

man Johnny Dodd.

under me. I believe it was the 6th of June 1944, the day of the invasion of Europe. I must have continued to go to the farm on my own, because the next memory I have, is Dad waking me and saying. "Get up, the war is over and we're having a street party." It was dark as he carried me down the road. When I asked him the time, he said, "About four o'clock, why?" "I want to go to the farm," I replied. "It's no use going to the farm yet, the cows are still in the field." "That's Okay," I'll see them milk the chickens," then started to explain how Mr Dodd had told me, before they milked the cows in the morning, they always milked the chickens first. I think this was to see if I could find their teats under their wings. Needless to say, Dad refused to let me go and retuned to the job in hand, which was to light a fire in the middle of the road, about half way down. This was done by people bringing out anything that would burn, including chairs, three piece suites and wardrobes, but when this ran out someone came up with the idea of taking the felt off the roof of the work's canteen, which was situated on land behind Station Green. They did this, but it then went on to the wooden roof, wooden doors and then the wooden sides. It was a bonfire that all tenants would remember, because the next day, the Unit Construction Co were out re-glazing the windows that had shattered with the heat the concrete road had cracked, the pitch expansion joints had melted and to say nothing of the disappearance of the work's canteen Mum once told me all the tenants had to pay a shilling a week extra on the rent for ten years to pay for the damage, but a good night was had by all.

That weekend Mrs Ledsham and a few other mothers organised tables and chairs to be put down the middle of the road for a street party. Nell Bowyer formed a choir and Flo Ellis, Bill Ellis's wife, arranged for games and competitions to be held in the small field at the bottom of the road, where Bill kept his donkeys, when they weren't working on the West Kirby Beach. Each family donated home-made cakes, tarts and other food, which was possibly a week's ration, out of their ration books, but they gave gladly, as us kids had seen very little party food in the last five years. I remember Mrs Briarcliff, bringing a plate out with pieces of fruit on it. They were round and about an inch long. "Do you know what this is Billy? If you can guess, you can have a piece." I didn't have a clue, "I don't know, Mrs Briarcliff' I said. "Oh Peter recognised it straight away." Peter was her son, a good lad but she always made him speak posh, coming from Wallasey on the Wirral, and she didn't shout to get him in, she clapped her hands gently and in would go Peter. Mind you, his dad was as scouse as they come, but he must have been a good engineer to have been working at the R.O.F.

"Peter recognised it, even in its yellow skin " Mrs Briarcliff said. "it's a banana Billy." The only banana I had ever seen was in a picture book. It was yellow, curved and hung in a bunch. It certainly wasn't round and an inch long, but Mrs Briarcliff was one of the best so she gave me a piece anyway.

It was now 1946 and I would be eight, just the right size to fit into a hole in the side of a stack of hay bales, where the hens laid their eggs. This meant me tunnelling into the hole, with a rope tied round my feet, picking up the eggs shouting "Okay," then being pulled out, feet first with the rope. I don't know if it was intentional, but on several occasions, the rope came loose, leaving me stranded in the hole, but I was always rescued one way or another. These bale's would be made up from the hay we had cut with the horse drawn mowing machine, using Jewel and Fashion to pull it. My job was to walk behind the mower with a hay rake, pulling the grass toward the blade and believe me, when you have walked round a six acre field for three hours at a time, you knew you'd done it. At first we would mow the grass and leave it in the swathes for about three days, then turn it over, using a turner pulled by one horse and after another day of sunshine, we would rake it into rows using an iron-wheeled horse drawn rake. Then came the hard bit. We had to cock it, this meant stacking it into small stacks which they called hay cocks. These would be about twelve feet apart, and raked smooth on the top to stop any rain from penetrating them. Later the cocks would be collected and stacked into a large stack, in the stack yard near the farm. This would cause the hay to sweat and the stack would give off a large cloud of steam, giving the impression of it being on fire. Some time later, Dave and Army Catton would come with there stationary baler and turn the whole stack into bales, but as time went on, Fred Lancaster came with his power take off pickup baler and did the whole operation on the field. During the harvest season it was my job to run out of school at 3.30pm, and collect the

Danny raking hay with Flower   Danny riding Fashion

bagging, from 29 Brails Berwick Road, which is where the Dodd's lived, and I would collect a bag of sandwiches from Colin's wife Molly, for the men working overtime that night. Molly was a lovely lady, she always put a separate parcel in with the name Bandy on it and it usually contained a piece of cake as well as sandwiches. But On one occasion I really blotted my copybook. Steve Sharps and Johnny Reed said they were going to climb the sandstone rocks from the railway line up to the park in Heath Lane. This meant running alongside the Little Sutton to Hooton railway lines, at the back of Berwick Road until we came to the sandstone cutting which had tree roots growing down. These enabled us to climb up the high embankment into the park, always known as the "Rec," due to it's official name, The Recreation Ground. This seemed too good an opportunity to miss, so I went along, completely forgetting the bagging for the men, who on that occasion went very hungry and thirsty. That took some living down, I'll tell you but I did manage to climb the sandstone rocks. 1946 was also the year I was

21

sent home from school because Mum was having a baby, but by the time I arrived, so had the baby, a little boy called Keith, later to be called "The Badger" due to the speed he could get under the chain link fence after being chased by Danny for playing football in the field. However, the practice paid off, because he played for Aston Villa, Birmingham City and Peterborough and Danny was always proud of him. I was told Mum had had a bad time at the birth as Keith was a twin, but the other twin didn't survive and Dr Greaves called for our Joyce to go upstairs as Mum was fading, but thank goodness, she survived and lived into her eighties.

Bruce outside of his kennel

Johnny racing Badger up
Pound Road

Willie Badger Ray

Home from the War

By this time, other people started to appear at the farm.
Margaret came home, Wilf and Collin returned from the
war and other friends of Danny's that had served in the
forces came to help. This made me feel very insecure, as
people started to treat me like a child, whereas old Mr
Dodd had always treated me like a man. What I soon
learnt was I couldn't get away with the same cheekiness
as I had with Mr Dodd. Wilf, who worked at the Shell
Refinery, helped most weekends on the farm and was
quite placid and would take some cheek off me. But he let
me know when enough was enough. Colin, who worked
for I.C.I. fertilisers, helped on the farm when he could, but
he was a firework. I remember once giving him cheek and
to my amazement, he picked me up and threw me across
the yard. Appealing to the boss for sympathy, I was told.
"Don't upset him, he has just spent five years fighting in
North Africa" Italy and up through Europe he's not going
to take cheek off a child is he?" After that, Colin became a

life-long fiend and I'm still in touch with his family.
Margaret worked for the Milk Marketing Board in Little
Sutton, behind Williams's dairy, who sold the best ice
cream in the county. She tested the milk from the local
farms for T.B, but her favourite pastime when she was on
the farm, was to catch me, strip me to the waist and
scrub me clean with cold water and Jeyes Fluid, which I
now admit I needed. She once said I had the same tide
mark round my neck for all of the six weeks summer
holidays. (I have no reason to doubt it).
Danny's mates, Arthur, Frank, Alf and Bryce, had another
way of what they called, " cooling my courage" This
entailed one holding my feet, another holding my hands,
three swings and into the pond I'd go. The pond was
about three feet of water and six inches of mud, so
although you could stand up, it was very difficult to walk
out. One of the most memorable occasions when this
happened was on a hot summers day, when Mum had
bought me a new vest! as we always got new vests and
wellies in the summer and new pumps "i.e. trainers" in
the winter, because they were cheaper out of season.
As I strutted across to the farm, I was full of confidence,
showing off my new vest, but very soon up to mischief.
Sure enough in the pond I went, screaming. "You can't
throw me in I've got my new vest on." With cries of
"sorry", they pulled me out, took off my vest, squeezed it
out, hung it on a nail to dry, then threw me back in!!!
Another time, Danny suggested I should learn to swim
and the way to do this was to put a long ploughing cord
round my waist and stand on one side of the pond. He

would then pull me across, whilst I kicked my legs and splashed my arms.. I slid down the bank up to my knees in mud and up to my shoulders in water. "Okay," I shouted, as Danny started to pull from the other side of the pond. All went well until I reached the middle of the pond, when the cord started to pull me down, instead of along. Gasping for breath, I shouted, "Help, help" and the louder I shouted, the harder Danny pulled, as he could see I was in trouble. But the harder Danny pulled, the deeper I went until he realised the cord was caught on a dead branch under the water. He then stopped pulling and I was able to stand up and walk out with both of us in fits of laughter. It goes without saying, those lessons stopped and I started to go to the open air Rivacre Swimming Baths. The baths were up to Olympic standard with full size diving boards, spring boards and were 14 feet deep at the deep end. But always cold, because it constantly circulated for hygiene purposes. I remember going with John Street school, one day a week in a single Decker coach for what they called Recreation and being handed a mug and an oxo cube. This was so after the swimming lesson when you had turned a funny colour of purple you could make yourself a hot drink on your way out, providing you could stop yourself shivering long enough not to spill it. Bearing in mind these lessons started about the fourth week in April. It was T, shaped with the bar of the T, being the children's paddling pool. It had two beautiful three-tier fountains, which you could sit in, while the water cascaded over you. The gardens were always well kept, the changing rooms clean and the picnic

Rivacre Swimming Baths

areas tidy. For such a small community this pool was amazing.

However, on the days us kids had no money, which was more often than not, we would swim in a pond called. "The fishy" on the now cultivated Rivacre Golf Course. This pond was clean and had a solid clay bottom due to being regularly dredged for golf balls when the golf course was in use before the war. Tom Unsworth, the farmer who now farmed the land as part of Stud Farm, ploughed, cultivated and sowed it with wheat seed. We thought this would stop us crossing the field, but to our delight he gave us permission to make one path to the pond, on the condition that if anyone strayed off the path, he would fill the pond with hawthorn branches. Needless to say, the bigger lads policed the path and it was kept open.

The other alterative was the Manchester Ship Canal, which was situated on the other side of Hooton Park. Having been a racecourse for training racehorses, hence the name Stud Farm, but was now a training airfield for the R.A.F. It is hard to believe in this day and age of health and safety and no-win-no fee claims, that we as kids, with very little education, but an abundance of common sense, were unofficially allowed to cross the runways. The rules were, if a flare was fired into the air, you cleared the runway and waited until a plane had taken off or landed. Then you legged it down the embankment to the third landing, just up from the Eastham Locks which takes the Manchester Ship Canal out to the Mersey.

One summer's day a gang of us, just entering our teens, went to swim at the third landing and one of the bigger lads, knowing I would rise to the bait, suggested, to become a man, I had to swim across the canal to Manisty's Mount. Of course I went for it, hook line and sinker. Because it was always me that was sent to get a left handed screw driver, a long rest a sky hook, or a shifting spanner that wouldn't shift. However on the way, I stood on a wasp's nest. I didn't realise what I had done until I felt a sting on the back of my neck, then on my legs. Suddenly, there was a swarm of wasps buzzing around my head. Frantically, swiping at them with my hands, I took off at full gallop across the airfield, not stopping, until I reached the canal and jumped in the water fully clothed at the third landing which was opposite Manisty's Mount, the place we intended to

The Fishy on the now renewed golf course, more natural now.

swim to. I stripped off my wet clothing as the other lads arrived. Then we all got into our swimming attire. This seemed to fall into three categories, borrowed trunks, home-made, or the ones knitted by your Mum, One lad told me his were made from parachute silk. I now realize, if I had undone the three stitches holding the crutch together, put my arms through the leg holes, I could have worn my trunks home as a V-neck jumper.

Manisty's Mount was the spoil from the diggings of the canal and separated the canal from the River Mersey. Legend has it, the charge hand navvy was a Mr Edward Manisty, so it became his mountain. All I knew was, once I swam from the third landing to Manisty Mount, I could call myself a man and that was my task for that day. I took off across the canal with other big lads nearby for support and safety. Making it across I was exhausted and had to hold onto the sandstone blocks, which were at the base of the Mountain, to rest. Now for the journey back. We set off slowly, until we reached the middle, then I looked to my left and saw a massive yellow bow heading towards me. It was a Shell Tanker. I put every ounce of effort into my swimming, but as the Tanker got nearer, it started to pull me towards it. As I fought against the current, I thought I was going under the ship, when suddenly, as it passed, the backwash shot me forward as though I was on a surfboard, planting me on the sandy bank of the third landing, safe and sound. We dried off, got dressed and made our way back, avoiding the wasps nest.

The Manchester Ship Canal

Not quite a Tanker

Keeping me busy

As I've said, we had a bull called Billy, a black and white Friesian with curved horns and two bulging eyes and whenever, he bellowed every back door on this side of Pound Road closed with a bang.
He had a ring in his nose, a steel mask over his face and a chain round his neck, attached to a railway sleeper, which he pulled around the field, but for all this, I had no fear of him. One very hot summers day, Danny and the lads were sunning themselves on the haystack and as usual, I was mythering for something to do. "Get the eggs

The Back field overlooking Pound Road as it is now Note the houses have now had sloping roves put on.

in from the hen shed," Danny said. Two minutes later, "Done that what now?" "Go and ask Jack the time and can we have a couple of long rests." In those days, when building hay stacks with loose hay, you sometimes had to put long planks of wood up the side of the stack to stop it leaning over, these were called long rests, also small fence posts were called short stays. Jack was a blind gentleman, who lived in one of the cottages, just down the lane and made his living making cane baskets and hampers. I did as I was told and ran down the lane, but couldn't figure out how Jack was going to be able to tell me the time if he couldn't see. I knocked on the big green shed door, which was in the cottage garden. "'Who is it?" Shouted Jack "It's Bandy, Mr Hughes," as I was never allowed to call him Jack. "Come in lad., what do you want?" "Danny said he needs a long rest and can you help by telling me the time?" Jack placed his hand in the right hand pocket of his waistcoat and produced a big silver pocket watch. Flicking it open with his right thumb, he placed his left hand over the fingers and said, "It's quarter past two and tell Danny, you've had a short stay and he's had all the long rests he's going to get. It's time to get back to work. "How did you see the time Mr Hughes?" I asked. "I didn't," he said, "I felt it with my fingers," then showed me the gold Braille face of the watch. I ran as fast as I could back up the lane to give Danny the message, but quickly followed it with, "What now?"
I don't know if Danny hadn't heard me, but Arthur said

"Oh go and get the bull in."
Following his instruction, I walked to Gibbon's field
where Billy was grazing. I opened the gate, walked up
to him, gave him a pat on his shoulder and undid the
chain from round his neck, put my fingers through the
ring in his nose and led him into his stall in the bottom
shippon, removed his mask, patted him again and
closed the door.
"Done that Arthur," "Done what?" Danny said,
overhearing the conversation, "I've got the bull in."
"What," Don't ever do that again. He could have
mauled you to death."
This put fear into me and the next day, when walking
across the field that Billy was in, he must have sensed
the fear, because he charged towards me and the
only place of safety was the pond, so in I went.
The reason we called it Gibbon's field was because Mr
and Mr's Gibbon's owned it and they lived in the nearest
of three big houses in Redlion Lane. Their relative
Mr Tomas Adam's came to live with them after returning
from war, and was affectionately known as the flying
officer, later to become the local Estate Agent.
Mr's Gibbons was very high up in the St John's
Ambulance Service. In the middle house was Mr and
Mr's Harden, a lovely couple with a son called John,
who helped me by giving me an open cheque to buy
an In pig Gilt at Leonard Wright and Co the cattle
market on Gorstacks in Chester, I paid him back with
thanks after the young pigs had been sold.
In the end house was Mr and Mr's Swindle of which I

know very little.

Just to prove I wasn't being bullied or picked on and didn't love every minute on the farm, I'll tell you about the time I joined the St Paul's Church choir.

I had to attend choir practice every Friday night. This was no problem, but getting there on a Sunday morning was, since I had to muck out the cows first. I then had to wash my wellies in the pond before running over the fields to St Paul's Church, which incidentally, Mr Dodd once told me, was a miniature of St Paul's Cathedral designed by Christopher Wren.

I attended for about three Sundays, then Mr Cook the Vicar, called me to one side and said. "Don't come again Billy, your wellies are causing me a problem," "Why Mr Cook?" I wash them before I come to church." "Yes Billy, but not high enough, because the cow muck at the top has turned the bottom edge of your white robe brown."

Talking of wellies, we had a very hot summer, so mum bought me a pair of white pumps size eight junior. These were great for going to school in, but were no good when mucking out the cows.

This is when Danny suggested I wear the white pumps inside a pair of wellies, size eight senior, so I did. However, I found the legs cut into my crotch. "No matter," he said "We'll turn them down" and as I walked away swinging the wellies with me, he said, "Come on Bandy Bill, now you can muck the cows out." That name stuck with me for life, as well I remember

St Paul's Church Hooton

being in my sixties at a rather posh charity do, when the main host, a very well known wealthy farmer stood up to speak and said, "How nice it is to see Bandy Bill here." "How are you Bandy? Haven't seen you for years." Rather than being embarrassed at being called Bandy, I stood up with pride and said "Very well Fred thank you how are you?"

I had known Fred Lancaster and fed him, with the bagging I had brought from Berwick Road at the age of nine, when he was just starting out as an agricultural contractor. At that time he had two tractors, a pickup bailer and a German Combine Harvester that Sid drove, earning him the nick name Heinz. Due to the shortage of farm implements after the war, Fred would hire or borrow a plough off one farmer to plough the field of another.

This proved to be a very good system as he prospered enough to move from a council tenant farm to buy one of the most prestigious farms in Ledsham.

However, time has moved on. Mr Dodd had been sick for some months and had passed away. Jewel had been sold and replaced by a Fordson Standard Tractor and a Shire horse called Flower.

I don't think I will ever forget the excitement when the tractor was unloaded off the trailer and I was allowed to sit on the springy cast iron seat. This feeling was soon dashed when I was told that the tractor would replace Jewel and Fashion.

It was a Thursday morning when Steven Peers came to pick up Jewel to take her to market. I remember to this day, the hurt as I sobbed floods of tears, because I couldn't go with her. I now realise it was for my own good, as she had gone for slaughter, as thousands of other Shires had at that time, due to tractors taking over. All that day at school I sat remembering the fun I had had catching her in

Radlands meadow, (which is now the practice range at the Rivacre golf club). Standing on the five bar gate to get on her back then holding her mane, giving her a friendly kick and off we'd go at full gallop down Truman's Lane, Redlion Lane and into the farmyard where she always knew to stop at the stables.

She was a very gentle, willing horse and would always help me harness her by putting her head down, so I could put the very heavy collar over her head, bearing in mind I was standing on a three-legged stool at the time. I also remember the time we had been carting muck on to the middle field with the two-wheeled muck cart and I was taking her out of the shafts, when the wheels rolled backwards trapping me under them next to Jewel's back feet, but she never moved until Danny arrived to lift them off me. Danny then sent me on the bus to Whitby Hospital where they found I had a broken thumb and then Danny complained, because I couldn't milk the cows due to my hand being in plaster.

The worst memory I have about Jewel is when Joe Benion, the blacksmith in Little Sutton, stopped shoeing horses and I had to ride her down Rossmore Road to the blacksmith in Ellesmere Port.

I rode her down Rossmore Road, past the Customs House, down the hill to the Grovenor pub and on up to Tilstons, the hardware shop, on past the Manchester House menswear shop, where later as a teenager, I would buy all the up to date shirts, ties and trousers. The Blacksmith's workshop was on the left, just before Carnegie Street, where we had the Majestic Ballroom and the Hippodrome Cinema, where again, as a teenager I would attend quite regularly. I took Jewel into the workshop and slid off her bare back and handed the bridle to the waiting blacksmith.

"Right," he said "Let's see whose boss."

Then he started to hit her with a large hammer shaft, although I strongly objected, being only eleven years of age, there wasn't a lot I could do to stop him, but believe me, when Danny took her for her second fitting he put the blacksmith wise.

Radlands Meadow

Three legged stool
milking can

Jewel, Danny and Johnny
Dodd

Iris helping the lads get the hay in on the Fordson
Standard Tractor

Six of the Best

I was now attending John Street secondary school in Ellesmere Port due to failing my eleven plus exams, but this didn't bother me at all, because I knew what I wanted and that was to work on a farm.

Me, Ray Gadsby, Johnny Reed and the other Unit kids caught the school bus at Rossmore Gardens, arriving at school ready for lessons at nine thirty a.m. The headmaster, was Mr Sturk, who lived in Berwick Road Little Sutton and we knew he would be keeping an eye on us, even in the holidays.

Mr Wright was the science teacher, but also the master of the Romans, which was one of four houses, the others being Celts, Saxons, and Normans, I was a Roman.

The system was, during the week, you would lose or gain

points for your house and be punished or rewarded at a house meeting on a Friday afternoon. It was mostly the former in my case.

I remember being in a mischievous mood one day when the maths teacher Mr Corium went out of the class for a few minutes. It came to mind to stick the wooden ruler in the hinge of the desk, dip a peace of blotting paper into the inkwell and flick it at the girl in front of me. Unfortunately, instead of it hitting her, it shot up and stuck to the ceiling above Corium's desk. Luckily for me it stayed there and nothing was said until later that afternoon.

It was Friday that day, the day we went to our house meetings, to find out who had lost or gained points, the punishment being one stroke of the cane on the hand for every three points lost.

I feel I must have been mischievous most of that week, as I had lost twenty points, which meant three strokes on each hand.

These I took like a man, without crying, then to my horror a lad came in and asked Mr Wright if the house master of the Celts Mr Corium could see Billy Bradley.

"What does he want?" I asked as we walked down the veranda to Corium's class. "You'll see, he said."

I walked in through the brown varnished door to a deafening silent class with all eyes on me.

"I believe this is yours Bradley," Corium said, holding a black ball of blotting paper between the fingers of one hand and a cane in the other. "Is it boy? Is it?" "Err yes sir."

"Yes Sir," he screamed, grabbing me by the coat collar. "Look what you've done to my register."

John Street Secondary School, centre windows was Mr Wright's class room.

The register was open on his table desk, with beautifully lined surnames of the children in his class. Black ticks for present, red crosses for absent, but in the middle, was a big black ink stain.

The paper had fallen from the ceiling on to his register. "Hold your hand out," he shouted. "No Sir, I've just had six on the hands." "Oh, we'll soon fix that," and he threw me over the desk, giving me six of the best, where it hurts most. One lad told me later Corium's feet left the floor as he swung the cane.

I walked back down the veranda biting my bottom lip to stop myself crying, when I met a girl I had always fancied and to my surprise, she put her arm round me and said. "Are you alright Billy you don't look well?"

That did it, the tears streamed as I ran back to Mr Wright's room to sit on the hot water pipes of the central heating at the back of the class to soothe my pain.

However, this didn't put me off girls and the way us lads impressed them was to make bracelets and necklaces by platting multicoloured wire that we had taken from the scrapped Spitfires and Hurricane aeroplanes parked along the North Road, which ran from Ellesmere Port to Eastharn Village. I remember a couple of girls saving their dinner money so that they could afford the bus fare to Little Sutton to see Ray and I.

This was Ann and Margaret but, sadly, Margaret passed away at a very young age after a childhood illness.

After many years, Ann and I met up again and my Wife Jean and our children became life - long friends with her husband Jim and their children and we enjoyed many good times together and are still in touch today.

Another childhood hobby was to collect army badges and put them onto your belt. The rarest ones were the Italian ones we got from the Prisoners of War at Ledsham Hall.

We did this by going to a pond called "The ten pits" on the Welsh Road and taking coots' eggs out of their nests and swapping them for badges with the Italian prisoners.

John Street Junior School

Learning the hard way

One weekend Wilf came to the farm and asked me if I
would load the two wheeled muck cart with cow
muck and deliver it to his house in Overpool I said I
would, using Fashion.
Now Fashion was nothing like Jewel. She was feisty and
rather than put her head down to help me put her
collar on, she would hold her head high to make it as
awkward as possible, but I always managed with the
help of a few cow nuts.
I loaded the cart and delivered the muck as asked.
But on leading Fashion home by the head we
reached the top of Rossmore Road, where they
were building the new Methodist Church.
The builders were using a very large diesel cement mixer
with a hopper to fill it.

As Fashion heard it pop-popping away, her eyes rolled and her ears twitched. "Steady," I said holding the bit in her mouth. "Steady old girl." Just then the hopper started to rise causing the mixer to pop even louder. She raised her head as the hopper went up. "Steady girl," I said again with my hands holding the bridle each side of her head.

Then to make sure the hopper was empty, the labourer hit it with a shovel. "Bang, Bang" it went. This is when Fashion took off at full gallop. I lifted my feet as high as I could and swung under her head.

Looking down, I could see her white ankle feathers, the pink hooves and the steel shoes as they struck the road. Holding on with all my strength I watched as we passed Station Avenue, Kings Road, then came to a stand still next to the Police Station at the Red Lion, only to be told by the old Cavalry man, Johnny Dodd, "Don't run her like that Bandy, you'll lather her up."

Little did he know it was Fashion who was lathering me up, not the other way round. I apologised to Johnny, as I had great respect for him and there was not a better horseman around than Johnny Dodd. I then turned Fashion round and walked her the half mile back to Station Avenue, where we should have turned off ten minutes earlier.

As I've said, Jewel was nothing like Fashion , as I well remember getting into trouble when Collin and Wilf took me down to Capenhurst Lane in Whitby to move their aunt out of a small cottage, using Jewel and the four wheeled rubber tyre'd flat trailer.

My job was to stand outside and watch Jewel while they dismantled the bed and rolled up the carpet inside. Auntie then came out and decided it was too cold for a little boy to be standing outside watching a horse and said I would be better inside having a cup of tea and a slice of cake. Naturally, I agreed and went in. I was just enjoying my cake when Collin said. "What are you doing in here?" "I'm having a piece of cake," I replied. "Then who's looking after Jewel?" "I am, I'll go out now and see to her."

I finished my tea and cake and went outside, but couldn't find Jewel. Not daring to go to Collin, I went to Wilf. "Have you moved Jewel, Wilf" 1 asked.

Wilf looked at me with surprise. "No, I haven't seen her I've been moving furniture around, Isn't she outside?." Wilf then ran to the end of the lane and looked down Pooltown Road, but could see no sight of Jewel.

He ran back to the cottage and took a bike from the shed and rode off, leaving me to face Collin. About an hour later he returned with Jewel and explained that he had found her standing outside the stable door at the farm. She must have felt she'd stood long enough outside the cottage and decided to go home. Again that took a bit of living down.

Mardin

Some time later Danny decided to have the new horse
Flower put in foal and a Welshman arrived with an
enormous bay stallion. The stallion was quite gentle, until
he saw Flower, who was obviously in season.
 That's when he started to whiner, buck, and stamp his
feet on the ash yard. "Come on old lad," said the
horseman, "Let's introduce you, so you can do your job."
Danny led Flower out of the stable towards the stallion
"There you go, Flower"
"What do you think of him"
The two horses weighed each other up. Flower attempted
to bite the neck of the stallion, but the stallion was having
none of it. Eventually, they calmed down and the
horseman led the stallion round to the rear of Flower, so
he could rest his head on her back.
After a short time the stallion started to attempt to mount
Flower, but found it difficult at first. This is when the
Welshman helped the stallion to enter, by balancing his
penis on his walking stick to guide him in. (That's the stallion
not the Welshman!!!.)

At this stage, I kept very quiet, because I had already had a clout round the ear off Margaret for commenting on how well the bull did when serving a cow.

I made the mistake of repeating what I'd heard one of the big lads say. "Orr, that's done her the world of good. That made her eyes water." That's when I got the clout.

The foal was born nine months later. Danny and I had sat for hours to see the birth, but horses are very shy in that respect. She foaled the very minute we went out to make a cup of tea.

The foal was a light brown colour with four white socks on his spindly legs. We named him Mardin, because he was so mardy i.e. "spoilt."

After a day or so, we turned Flower and her foal out into a field, known as the brickie, due to part of it being where they had dug out clay for brick making in the brick works at the bottom of Rossmore Road.

We watched them both prosper and shine in the summer sun until one day, about six months later, to our horror, Mardin was found hanging between two boughs of a tree, next to a ditch.

He had been rubbing his neck between the boughs and the bank had given way under his feet, causing him to drop down into the ditch and choke to death.

Everyone was heart-broken as we cut down one of the tree boughs to release him, so we could bury him in the field.

The one and only time I ever saw a horse foal was when walking past Bill Ellis's field and a pony was in full foal. The foal came out in a skin bag and was rolling round and kicking inside, until the pony got up and bit a hole in the bag, releasing the foal.

She then started to lick the foal dry and very shortly after, the youngster was on his unsteady feet, suckling from his mother's teats. A sight to be seen. I'd seen plenty of cows calve, but the one that springs to mind is Clover.

One afternoon, when bringing the cows in to milk, I noticed Clover had an extra large udder and the teats were dripping milk. "What's wrong with Clover?" I asked Danny. "Oh, she'll calve today for sure," he said. We chained the cows up in their stalls, washed their udders and carried on with the milking. When all the other cows had been milked Danny said.

"Put the cows back in the field, but leave Clover in, she'll calve soon." We mucked out the shippon "i.e. cowshed," washed down the dairy, put the hens in the shed and put the chain on the field gate. Then we were all ready for home. All was well, except Clover hadn't calved. Danny suggested I went home for something to eat and come back later.

I ran home and grabbed anything that would fit between two slices of bread, so as not to waste time and miss anything.

On the way back I met my mate Ray, who said he would like to see Clover calf, so off we ran across the field to the farm. By this time, Danny had called the vet out, Jimmy Twysell, a red headed Scotsman.

Jimmy placed his hands either side of the crown of

Clover's tail and said.

"The bones have gone, I'll have a feel around."

He stripped to the waist and soaked his arms with a large bar of carbolic soap, which was next to the bucket of cold water.

Pulling Clover's tail to one side, he slowly pushed his hand into Clover's womb. "I think there's two in here and one is above the other, she'll need a caesarean. I'll get my bag." Jimmy went to his car and returned carrying a brown leather bag, a bottle and a wad of cotton wool.

"Are you two here to help?" "Yes Mr Twysell," we said in unison. "Right now watch what I do," He opened the bottle and poured out some liquid onto the cotton - wool, then started to dab it on to Clover's nose. "Stand back" he said. "She'll go down in a minute." Sure enough down she went. "Okay, Bandy, you hold the bottle and the cotton - wool and keep dabbing it onto her nose" I dabbed for a few minutes, but was more interested in what was happening behind me. So I said to Ray.

"Here you are Ray, you have a go." Ray took the bottle and with all his enthusiasm poured more liquid onto the cotton — wool. This gave me the opportunity to watch Jimmy pull one calf out of the incision he had made in Clover's side.

The calf was wet and slimy, but breathing okay. So I got the job of rubbing it down with wads of straw, while Jimmy pulled out the other calf, which was also okay. Jimmy then started to sow the wound on Clover's side, but noticed Ray had gone very quiet. "Hello Ray, are you alright? Ray! Ray! Oh dear he's out cold." Jimmy said.

Jimmy then started to explain that Ray had got too close to the chloroform, but would be alright, when he'd slept it off.

Danny then carried Ray and put him on some hay bales, waiting for him to wake up, with no doubt one king size headache.

In the meantime, Jimmy finished sowing up Clover. I finished rubbing down the calves and Danny was pleased to have added two beautiful Friesian calves to the herd.

While we were waiting for Ray to wake up and to get over the ordeal of Clover, Danny and I stood, looking out of the big shippon window across the Rivacre Valley, where we could see the gold of Norman Dodd's wheat crop when Danny said. "Take a good look at that sight Bandy, one day it'll all be houses." As indeed it now is.

The Open Road

Norman Dodd was Danny's cousin and farmed two
farms in Rivacre Road along with his brother
Charlie. They supplied most of Ellesmere Port and
Little Sutton with milk from a horse drawn cart.
Another school mate of mine, Barry Stout, known as
Bass, worked before school and at weekends with
Margie, on the bottle washer. This washed all the
returned empty milk bottles, ready for refilling and
redelivery.
A courtship started and some years later Barry and
Margie married, had two lovely children Kevin and
Louise, who became life long friends of my children.
One day, Bass and I were in school comparing notes as to
what we were doing on the farms over the weekend.
I told him we were muck carting. "Muck spreading you
mean" Bass said. "No muck carting, We fill the two
wheeled horse drawn muck cart with muck, take it to

53

the field and put small mounds every six yards and go
back later and spread it." I replied.
"What a waste of time, You've got a tractor haven't you?"
"Yes Bass we have."
."Well Norman has a muck spreader, All you do is fill it
with muck, put it behind the tractor and it spreads as it
goes along."
I said "That sounds great! Do you think he'd lend it to
us when he's not using I will ask him tomorrow Bandy
and let you know."
A few days later Bass came up with the good news.
Norman would lend us the muck spreader each
weekend, providing, we collected and returned it by
Monday morning.
I rushed home and told Danny we could have the muck
spreader for the weekend and to my amazement he said.
"Right Bandy you can collect it straight after milking on
Saturday morning."
"Me?! " I said "Yes you'll be okay, put my big coat on, pull
up the collar and wear that trilby hat hanging on the wall.
Powly will never know it's you."
Powly was the local Bobby, who worked at the police
house and station at the top of Red Lion Lane and only
twelve months earlier, had been seeing me over New
Chester Road, to get to Berwick Road junior school.
Now, the possibility arises that he could very easily
overtake me on his bike and arrest me for underage
driving. Anyway, I set off down the lane, through the Unit
and on to Rossmore Road, heading for Norman's farm. I
was dressed, as described earlier, driving a Fordson
Standard Tractor, travelling at about five miles per hour

flat out, but proud as punch.

I collected the spreader and returned to Danny's farm, where he had already pulled out of the shed, the four wheeled haywain, and said.

"That's where the spreader is going tonight. If it rains, it's our tackle that gets wet, not the tackle we've borrowed." That's stuck with me all my life. Always look after someone else's property, more than your own.

This brings to mind the time we borrowed a tent to go camping down the valley. It was a small brown ridge tent, meant to sleep two adults, but by head and tailing, it would take four kids easily.

We set off with my trusted dog Tricks, down to the Rivacre Brook and pitched the tent. Tricks was the little brown puppy that Dad had bought off Aunty Reanie's friend, as a pure bred Alsatian, but had grown up to be a very obedient, gentle mongrel with a curled up tail. Nonetheless, we lit a small camp fire and scraped a hole in the bottom of the stream. We waited for the silt to settle, took water from the hole, made a brew and ate the bread and cheese I had taken from the pantry at home. As night fell, the mist started to rise, but we didn't mind. We were snuggled under the blanket I had taken off the bed at home.

We giggled and made jokes for some time, then fell asleep, only to be woken by voices shouting, "Billy where are you?" "Billy are you there."

On recognizing Mum's and our Jean's voices, I scrambled out of the tent and peered into the mist. "I'm here Mum, over here in the tent." Mum's silhouette appeared through the mist.

"Why didn't you tell anyone you were going camping?, I thought you were lost."

"No Mum, I'm alright, I'm with my mates and we've got Trick's."

Mum was working as a barmaid at the Railway Inn, which at the time stood at the junction of Heath Lane and New Chester Road in Little Sutton. She worked llam until 3pm, came home, then worked 5.30pm to 10. 30pm, in summer time getting home about 11pm. Of course, this night she'd arrived home to find I wasn't there, but this had happened many times before. On one occasion, after Midnight, she found me wandering up Pound Road, holding a paraffin lamp saying. "I had to stay at the farm late because a cow was calving."

Then she kept me up even later, telling her how we had to soap our hands and arms to put the calving ropes round the calf's front feet to help pull it out.

Or the night we turned our Dougie's pigeon shed into a den and slept in it, that night I could hear Mum arguing with Dad saying. "Leave them alone they'll be alright."

To say nothing of the time we spent in the underground dugout den in the

Bricky. This was a hole dug in the clay with cut-out steps going down into it. We then covered it over with tin sheets, covered the sheets with soil, dug small holes in the side for holding candles, then cut out a bigger hole in which we made a fire.

The drawback to this was, when the fire was lit, the big lads would put grass sods on top of the upturned bottomless bucket which acted as a chimney and this would bring us out coughing and spluttering, then gasping for air.

Bill I his red silk shirt bought from the Manchester house

Trix in the Rivacre Vally

Dave Hugie Bass Trix

Hugie Bill Dave Tri-x

Bill the Boxer

One day, Bass rode down from Queens Road Little
Sutton where he lived, after being brought up on
Sillcocks fairground, which had found itself trapped in
Ellesmere Port at the outbreak of war.
I was told that, due to the bright lights, fairgrounds
were ordered to stop travelling, so although Sillcocks
were based in Fleetwood, they had to stay at the top of
Westminster Road, Ellesmere Port for the duration.
This delighted the public, because what they did was,
cover the complete show with tarpaulin sheets and
made it an indoor fairground, which could be opened on
occasions, providing there were no air-raid warnings.
Bass had rode down on a brand new Hercules bike. It
was green in colour with straight handle bars, a bell,
three speed gears, a pump and two leather pannier
bags on the back.
Getting hold of the handlebars, I said. "That's fabulous

Bass, can I have a go?

Handing it over with some reservations he said. "Yes but don't fall off and scratch it."

I cocked my leg over the crossbar and rode it half way down Pound Road and back. "Smashing," I said, handing it back to him. "Are you going to school on it?"

"No, but I'm going to stay with Uncle Abe on Sillcocks fair in the holidays.

If you can get a bike you can come with me."

The next morning when Danny and I were milking, I mentioned what Bass had said and to my surprise, Danny offered to lend me the boss's bike, which hadn't been used since he'd died. "Great", I said, "when can I have it?"

"Pick it up tomorrow and ride it to school to see if it suits you."

The following day, I went to Danny's house in Berwick Road and met Molly, Collin's wife.

"Hello Molly, I've come for the boss's bike. Is that Okay?"

"Yes, it's in the shed," she said, opening the black door of an outhouse. As she reversed the bike out by the seat, I could see it wasn't a Hercules, mainly because it was black and not green, but it was also a lady's bike. It had curved handlebars, black hand grips, and a bell on the right hand side, a little leather bag with a multipurpose spanner, and puncture outfit inside, and a front and rear hand brake. The frame had no cross bar, which allowed ladies in long dresses to put one leg either side of the pedals, before starting to ride.

The back mudguard had holes in, an inch apart, on each side with strings threaded through, going to the centre cog of the wheel. This was to stop the ladies dresses catching in the wheel, Molly explained. Nonetheless, it was a bike and I rode it home with pride.

The next day, I told the lads I wasn't getting the bus to school, but riding the bike for practice.

I set off early that morning with my pants tucked into my socks, arriving at school on time, waiting for the lads to arrive on the bus.

That evening the lads challenged me to beat the bus to Rossmore Gardens, where they would be getting off.

I took up the challenge and set off before they had entered the bus.

Pedalling as fast as I could down Rossmore Road, I could hear them cheering as the bus passed me by.

I arrived a few minutes later, where the lads were waiting for me, along with some other kids that had got off the bus, one being Kenny Rogers.

"Ah you lost," he said, and for some unknown reason pushed me off the bike.

"What did you do that for?" I asked.

"Because I felt like it" he said. "What are you going to do about it?" Not knowing if I could beat him in a fight I thought it best to stay calm and go on my way with the lads.

Suddenly, he snatched the bike from my hands and threw it into the brambles on the side of the Council rubbish tip.

I felt a rage build up in me, not for what he'd done to me, but for what he'd done to the Boss's bike.

I rushed forward with my arms flailing like a windmill. "A

fight, a fight," someone shouted, and everyone formed a circle round us.

In those days every fight was a fair fight or so you hoped. The two people concerned would fight until one gave in. Then the other claimed to be the winner.

No one else in the crowd would get involved, because this would leave you open to the claim you were helped.

I pushed forward hoping to score a blow, but to no avail, only to receive a right hook to my left ear, then another to the stomach.

I still went forward with the hope of grabbing his arms and wrestling him to the ground. This only resulted in me receiving more punishment to the head. The only thing I can say is, I kept going forward, but every step cost me dearly. We fought through the nettles and brambles. I could feel the tingling in my legs, as the thorns cut into my trousers. My hands were red with nettle stings.

Rogers, then looking as exhausted as I felt said. "Give in, or I'll hit you again."

Having none of it I said, "Never."

Bang, I then felt my nose explode, my eyes water and I could taste the blood as it ran into my mouth.

The next thing I remember, was being held back by a bus driver, who had jumped from his bus to stop the fight.

Holding me behind his back, the driver said to Rogers "On your way lad, this one's had enough."

Leading me back through the nettles the driver picked up my bike and said. "Get off home and clean yourself up."

I called in the house and swilled my face, but then went straight to the farm to tell Danny the story.

After a short while he suggested I join the Star Boxing

Club, run by Trevor Brassier in the loft of the Boathouse Pub.

The Boathouse was on the side of the Shropshire Union Canal in Ellesmere Port and Trevor had kitted it out with a boxing ring, punch bag, medicine balls and skipping ropes.

Trevor owned and ran a local car sales and mechanic's garage with his brother, but was also an amateur boxer. I joined and attended for a few weeks, but I must admit it didn't turn me on, so after a short time I gave it up.

Danny, not being a person to let me get away with things, brought a pair of boxing gloves in one day and said.

"Fill a sack with straw, hang it from a beam and practice on that."

Putting on the gloves, I sparred around, making lots of swishing sounds from my mouth and snorting through my nose like the lads had done in the boxing club.

But it wasn't for me, I just had no interest whatsoever.

One very wet day, Danny, Ray and I, found ourselves with nothing to do, so Danny suggested, Ray and I have a boxing match and he would score the points.

The problem was, we only had one pair of gloves. Answer "Have one each." We put on the glove, me the left, Ray the right.

Then we tucked our spare hand into our belt behind our back and fought three rounds, Ray winning on points.

Ray and I both knew he could beat me, but we were great mates, so it didn't matter. I wouldn't call him a fighter, but he could certainly handle himself. The only time I ever saw Ray in trouble was when he had an argument with

posh Peter Briarcliff and Peter said, "If you don't stop arguing Raymond, I shall bop you on the nose."
Ray continued and Peter did exactly what he said he
would do, bopped him on the nose. Ray gasped in
amazement as Peter said.
"I'm sorry Raymond, but I did warn you."
The two lads shook hands and that was that.
I also sparred with a lad named Willy Roberts in the same
fashion and to this day, he still tells people how he beat
me on points, with one hand tied behind his back.

The Eccentric Welshman

Earlier that month the sow had farrowed, having thirteen piglets, seven of which were hogs and were now ready for castrating. The thirteenth was a small undernourished pig and had to be put into a tea-chest for it's own safety.

The castrating was carried out by an eccentric Welshman called Taffy Lloyd, who lived in the big black and white house near the old Black Lion Pub. The house had stables, from where Taffy bred, trained and raced high-stepping trotters.

These were ponies that ran with their legs in tandem and pulled two wheeled traps. Taffy would drive the pony round a racetrack against other competitors and was very successful at it because the stable walls were covered in First place rosettes.

Danny sent me to ask Taffy if he could call and castrate the pigs, but on the way back, I called to see two other school mates Kenny Donson and Arthur Bell, who lived just behind the Black Lion Pub.

Arthur later changed his name and became Steve Vierdor the very well respected wrestler and TV personality.

I stayed for about half an hour, then made my way home down Black Lion Lane, where I met Lenny Lloyd (no relation to Taffy) and a group of other lads sitting on a massive tyre.

"Hello lads what's going on?"

"We've got to get rid of this tyre" Lenny replied.

"I'll take it. We may be able to use it on the farm."

Lenny then instructed me and the other lads to lift one side of the tyre. Up it went and to my surprise, it was higher than me and stood up on it's own.

"Where are you taking it?" Lenny asked.

"If you'll give me a hand, I'll take it home today and on to the farm tomorrow."

We wheeled it through the village, one in front and one behind to stop it running away from us, as we wheeled it down Red Lion Lane to our house. The next morning I ran across to the farm and told Danny that Taffy would be coming about half past ten to castrate the pigs. "Okay," he said "lets turn the sow out."

Danny stood behind a plywood board to push the sow out of the pigsty, leaving the young on their own.

We then put fresh straw in a clean sty and waited for

Taffy.

Ten thirty came and went and as usual the eccentric Welshman turned up late.

But when he did turn up, he was in a pony and trap.

The pony looked very undernourished and the once beautiful trap was held together with bale wire.

I asked Danny what had gone wrong and he explained that Taffy had lost his wife after a very long illness and therefore, suffered long bouts of depression, leading to him neglecting his ponies at times.

I tied the pony to the stack-yard gate and gave it a feed of hay, then walked back to the pigsty where Taffy was sharpening his curved castrating knife. Danny commented on the state of the pony and promised to call at least three times a week to check on Taffy and his stock, which he did until Taffy passed away.

"Come on Bandy it's time you learnt how to castrate a pig." Danny said. "Okay what shall I do?"

"Grab one of the hogs by the back legs, put your back against the wall and swing his head between your legs and hold him there."

I am now in amongst twelve piglets trying to identify the hogs from the gilts and then catch one.

Finally, I succeed and end up against the wall holding a 201b. pig, (10kilo) upside down kicking and squealing for all it's worth, with it's mother outside squealing and chewing at the door trying to get back in.

Taffy felt between the pig's legs and selected a testicle, pulled it tight against the skin and made a cut about an inch long.

Out popped a small round ball on a skin cord which Taffy cut, then threw the ball into a nearby bucket. At this point, I thought Taffy would cut the second ball, but no, he then takes out of his pocket a stick of chewing tobacco and cuts off a slice with the very same blood stained knife he had used on the pig. Popping the tobacco into his mouth, he then cut the second ball and discarded it into the bucket, spread some antiseptic salve onto the wound and said. "Okay Bandy, put him back into the clean sty and get me another."

This was repeated six more times and believe me, although my testicles were aching like the rest of my body, I did appreciate the fact that I still had them!.

We then let the sow back in, to allow her to settle them down. As for the writ, I asked Danny if I could take it home, but due to the fact I had taken one home before and it had died in the kitchen, he suggested we keep it in the shippon where it was warm and could be bottle fed.

We nursed it for a week or so, until it could drink milk out of a saucer, then a small pan, then a bucket.

We named her Mertal and she followed us round like a dog, until one day we went thinning out turnips and she decided to help by rooting up every plant she could find. This is when Danny said she would have to be fastened into a pigsty, where she cried like a baby for a week.

When I got home that day, I found a group of kids sitting on the tyre outside our house. "Where did this come from Bandy?" someone asked. "Me and Lenny Lloyd brought it from the Black Lion." "What for?" came the reply.

"I'm taking it to the farm to see if Danny wants it. Will you give me a lift with it?"

We all lifted together and up came the tyre standing proudly on it's own.

"Come on," I said. "Lets roll it down the road to the farm." Suddenly, I think it was Johnny Reed, found he could straggle the tyre and it would take him up and over.

The next to try was me, then Ray and before long half the kids in the road were running alongside the tyre taking it in turns to go up and over. This proved to be too good a game to lose, so we turned the tyre round and pushed it back to our house.

After some practice we found that as many as four of us could stand upright on top of the tyre and walk it along the road.

But without a doubt, the best trick was to curl up inside it and get the rest of the kids to roll you as fast as they could down the road.

The downside to this was that the best way to stop it, was to hit the tree at the bottom of the road by Jimmy Wraight's house.

The best kid at this game was our Jean because not only was she small and light, but when she hit the tree she would fall out of the tyre, saying. "That was great, can we do it again," and she would push the tyre up the road herself.

Unfortunately, after a few months a couple of the more so -called responsible parents deemed it too dangerous and threw the tyre into the Newt pond in the Bricky field, where I think it stayed until the field was built on.

Johnny Lenny Albert in the Bricky field

Johnny at the Newtie pond

Johnny in the Bricky

Johnny and Bill in the Bricky

The Big Ride

That summer holiday Bass asked me if I was still interested
in going with him to stay with his Uncle Abe on Sillcocks
Fair.
"Yes," I replied. "When are we going and what will I need?"
"We'll leave early Saturday morning when the roads are quiet
and you'll need a change of clothes and a packed lunch."
This to me meant a second shirt and a bag of jam butties,
which I stuffed into a shopping bag and tied it behind the
seat of the bike.
I arrived at Bass's house about six o'clock on the Saturday
morning, where he was waiting with his panniers packed
tight and map in hand.
"Are you ready? Then lets go," he said.
We started off up Redlion Lane and turned right towards
Birkenhead, all went well for the first few miles until Bass
mentioned we were going on the ferry to Liverpool.
"Why is that?" I asked, "I thought the fair was in Ellesmere

Port."

"No it's moved to Fleetwood."

"Fleetwood where's that?"

"Just the other side of Liverpool," came the reply.

"Liverpool, that's miles away."

The only time I had ever been to Liverpool was when
Mum had taken us to New Brighton for a day out.
This meant us getting a green bus, a blue bus, two ferry
boats and a yellow bus, "Liverpool wow."

Nonetheless, we pushed our bikes onto the ferry at
Woodside, crossed the Mersey and disembarked at the
Pier Head in Liverpool.

We rode over the cobble stones of the Dock Road
passing all the tall cranes feeding the ships moored in
the docks on the River Mersey.

Then we joined Scotland Road where I had to stop at a
bike shop to try and borrow a piece of string, as the
shopping bag was now rubbing on the side of my wheel.
Imagine a twelve year old country bumpkin up against
the wit and humour of a Scouse shop keeper as he tries
to borrow a piece of string -no chance! "Borrow? A piece
of string? We sell things here you know, that's how we
pay the rent."

"Ere, yes sir, how much will it be?" I said quivering in my
boots.

The man turning to his colleague in the shop said. "Do
you think this lad has enough money to buy a piece of
string?."

"I doubt it, it's very expensive these days, isn't it?" he
replied.

The first man then fired a barrage of questions at me. "How long is a piece of string? How thick? What colour? What's it for? Why do you need it? "

"My bag keeps falling onto the wheel of my bike and slowing me down and I've got to get to a place called Fleetwood by tonight."

"Fleetwood on that" said the second man, bring it into the shop and we'll see what we can do."

The two men set about tying up the bag and making it secure. They renewed the brake blocks on the back wheel, oiled the chain, then patted me on the back and wished me well.

Not a penny changed hands as I went on my way to catch up with Bass, who was waiting some yards up the road

Turning right, we joined the A 59 for Ormskirk, which I remember very well, because it was flat and a dual carriage way, which I had never seen before. What struck me more, was the lack of fencing in the fields, but then I realised there were no cattle in them, just potatoes and vegetables as far as the eye could see. (I now know Ormskirk is the garden of Liverpool.) About this time I started to ask Bass where exactly Fleetwood lay and at what time did he think we would get there. His reply was very vague "It's at the end of this road," he replied.

On reaching Preston we had a long chat about which was the shorter distance, to go home, or to go on. We chose the latter and pushed on along the Golden Mile of Blackpool promenade, which by this time was lit up and in full swing.

I concentrated as hard as I could to keep my bike wheels out of the tram lines, as I gazed in amazement at the sites, such as the big wheel, the flashing lights of the fair ground and the Blackpool Tower.

Finally we saw a sign "Welcome to Fleetwood." We then made our way through the narrow streets to Victoria park, where to my delight we found Sillcocks Fairground.

"Come on Bandy, lets go and find Uncle Abe," Bass said pushing his bike into the darkness behind the stalls. This is where the mobile homes were parked. So we looked round until we found a large caravan and knocked on the door.

A dark haired thin faced chap opened the door as Bass said "Hello Uncle Abe it's Bass, Jack's lad, we've come to stay the week."

"Oh there's two of you are there?" Abe said. "The best place for you two is in the generator wagon."

This was a four - wheeled flat nosed box wagon, which housed a generator that filled the whole of the back. It had large doors at the rear and a small door on the side, which Bass and I crawled through.

Once inside, we found it very hot next to the generator. It was very dark and it had a wooden floor, but after a sixteen hour bike ride it felt like, what I would imagine, a five star hotel feels like, not ever having visited one!!

The following day the fair ground stayed closed due to it being Sunday, so this gave Bass and I ample time to walk round Fleetwood and see the sights. I emphasise "walk," because the last thing I wanted was to even see a bike, let alone ride one.

On the Monday morning, Abe invited us to help set up his two stalls, which were a shooting gallery and coconut shy. What we had to do was to make sure we had plenty of prizes on the shelves and all the guns were chained to the counter.

In the case of the coconut shy, it was plenty of prizes, four big bags of sawdust and plenty of wooden balls in the boxes behind the counter.

Then the music started to play, the rides began to turn, and the people started to flood in.

"Don't just stand there," Abe shouted. "You're on the guns Bass and you come with me."

I followed Abe to the coconut shy, where he showed me how to put the coconuts onto the stands. The stands were steel pipes about three feet high with a soup — like dish welded on top.

The idea was to put a handful of sawdust in the dish then place a coconut onto the sawdust and allow people to throw wooden balls, with the hope of knocking off a coconut to win a prize.

Abe started to take the money and the balls started to fly. The biggest problem for me was to dodge the balls as I tried to replace the coconuts that were falling thick and fast.

After a short time and a lot of prizes being given away, Abe asked me to show him how I was putting the coconuts up. "Like this" I said, piling up the sawdust and balancing the coconut on top. "No wonder they're all winning, you could blow them off with a good puff of wind with the amount of sawdust you're using." "Sorry Abe," I said.

"This is the way to do it," Abe explained. "Let the punter see you put the sawdust on, then as you draw the coconut back, push it off again this makes it harder to knock the coconut off.

I took the lesson to heart and did as I was told, but felt very guilty for a short time.

But, there again, if I'd have had my way every punter would have won.

Over the next four days I worked with Bass and Abe between the guns and the coconut shy, having the time of my life now my backside had stopped smarting, but I wasn't looking forward to the bike ride back.

Then came a blessing from heaven. One of the stall-holders said he was going to Warrington to get some swag and tack (prizes) and would Bass and I like a lift that far.

The only drawback was that we would have to leave on Friday, not Saturday. It took us all of two seconds to decide and we accepted his offer with gratitude.

Friday morning came and we loaded our bikes into the stall-holders van, but were very disappointed at having to leave the fair.

We said our goodbyes to Abe and his family and thanked him for his hospitality.

Climbing into the van, the stall holder (sorry can't remember his name) said, "Will it help being dropped off at Warrington?"

"It sure will," Bass replied. We'll only have to ride to Helsby and we know our way home from there."

I sat behind the driver's seat and slept most of the way back, but woke up to hear the driver say. "If you know your way from Helsby, I may as well drop you there and it will give you a good start home."

It must have been just after midday when he dropped us at Helsby.

Thanking him, we unloaded our bikes and set off on the last few miles past the Shell Refinery, thinking what an exiting experience this country bumpkin had had over the past week.

Bass and Bill in Bass's garden   Bill in Victoria Park Fleet wood

Suttons Barmy Army

Then came the winter, the frost froze the "Fishy" and it became the perfect skating rink, until the day I went through the ice and Nigel Hughes pulled me out. I was absolutely freezing, so Nigel suggested he would take me home. On the way home, the conversation went from how he had pulled me out, to how he had saved my life and he felt he deserved a reward.

We crossed the fields and arrived at the back door of our house, just as my Mum came out.

"What's happened to you," she said.

"I fell through the ice Mum." Then Nigel butted in and said.

"I've just pulled Bandy out of the Fishy and saved his life. Is there a reward?"

"Reward?" Mum screamed, as she swung her right hand connecting with Nigel's left ear. "The chances are you threw him in, in the first place, get on your way you cheeky little B!!!"

But for all his cheek, Nigel didn't do too badly he ended up owning and running two high class Jewellers one shop in Ellesmere Port and the other in Chester.

When the snow came we all made sledges out of anything we could find such as wooden fences and the like. The runners would be 3"x1" timber chamfered at the front with metal strips nailed to the bottom to make them slide. We even had the window cleaner's ladder from Queens Road, chamfered at the front. This was great,   because as many as six could sit on it at once to go down the "Roly Poly Hill".

The best was the pram frame Johnny Ledsham had. He took the wheels off a pram, which left it with chrome-plated runners, leaving everyone else standing. He could go down the "Roly", under the fence and across Rossmore Road. Then we decided to go to the Rivacre Valley. This was a long slope down, where you could end up in the Rivacre Brook, if you weren't careful.

But the more braver or stupid of us went down the "Killer".

This was a long slope but half-way down, the hill fell away fast, which meant the sledge left the ground for some ten yards before touching earth again, three quarters of the way down. A ride to remember.

As the seasons changed and spring became summer, Tony Hall talked us into joining the Army Cadets at Childer Thornton.

This was run by Lt Bill Walters and RSM Bill Jacks. The drill shed was in the field opposite St Paul's Vicarage which are now housing estates. Bill Walters ran the petrol station in Little Stanney and Bill Jacks was a retired gentleman from Hawthorn Road, Little Sutton. Both were good lads and kept us well trained and safe.

In 1952 we went on a week's camp to Cark in Cartmel near Grange-overSands, Cumbria, where all the Army Cadet forces from the North West met to drill and do field training.

The drill squads were picked and competitions held between each company, ready for the finals to be held at Abbots Park drill hall in Chester. The first prize was the Saunders Cup, which the winners kept for twelve months.

Back at the camp, we drilled and did field training most of the days, but my most vivid memory is the night we went to Grange-Over-Sands.

We were told it was a fishing village, which specialized in shrimping and were advised to sample the shrimps whilst we had the opportunity.

Ray and I headed for the beach and very soon realised where the name came from. The sands stretched for miles before reaching the sea.

We walked on and very soon came across some ladies who were sitting at benches head and tailing shrimps. "Hello can we buy some shrimps?" I asked. "Yes," replied a lady.

"Shelled or Not shelled?"

"What's the difference?" Ray said.

The lady then informed him it was cheaper if we shelled them ourselves. "Okay we'll have half a crown's worth," (although now, only twelve and a half pence, in 1952 it would buy two seats into the pictures and an ice-cream.)

The lady set about putting shrimps into a newspaper with a small silver shovel until they were piled high and handed them to Ray.

"Thanks," he said and we started to walk away.

"Just a minute you haven't got yours yet."

She then handed me the same amount as she had given Ray.

We then started the long walk back before deciding to sit on a wall to eat our shrimps. This we did, by cracking the shell, pulling off the head and popping the remainder into our mouths.

Very soon we had both had enough and were feeling very sick. We discarded the remainder of the shrimps into a nearby waste bin, before heaving the ones we'd eaten into a grid on the side of the road, (half a crown poorer.)

The trip to Grange-Over-Sands proved to be worthwhile because that year with the help of Tony Hall, John Watson and one or two others we won the Saunders Cup at Abbots Park and proud we were too.

On returning to the farm, I asked Danny if I could rent the small woods next to our house, so I could keep some pigs of my own. To my delight he agreed, but on the condition I fenced it off and it was rent free.

Bob Davies, a farmer from Childer Thornton, told Danny I

Left front, Terry, John, ?? rear Left, Eric, Tommy, Tony.
Little Sutton squad in the Saunders Cup at Abbots Park
Chester

could have the pig wire from around his field, if I took it
down myself.

We set about taking out the staples, rolling up the wire,
relocating it round the oak trees, next to our house and
built a small tin shed as a shelter for the pigs.

I then bought two young gilts off Danny and named
them Girt and Elsie after mine and Ray's mum. My
intention was to put the gilts to the boar when ready, but
due to a shortage of finance, I sold them off as porkers,
banking the money in the Nat West Bank in Little Sutton.
Some time later, I was told Chester Races were on and I
asked Ray if he fancied going. He agreed and to the great

The Ellesmere Port and district Army Cadet's at Grange-Over-Sands. Front row left first in RSM Bill Jacks, third in, Lt Bill Walters In the middle Colonel Offley

Second row right, second in Tony Irving, third in Ray Gadsby. Third row right, fifth in Bill Bradley sixth in Dave Blisit.

dismay of a lovely bank clerk from Rosmore Gardens, I drew all but one pound out of the bank and lost the lot at the races.

I had many tries after that, but even with the kind people who helped me with finance and labour, I just couldn't make the pig trade pay.

The next time I went to the Chester Racecourse was when

the Cheshire Show was held there.

I managed to acquire two tickets from Jones's Meal Merchants from Mollington and a couple of vouchers for food and drink from Burgesses, the agricultural merchants on Cow Lane Bridge in Chester.

Ray and I set off by bus to Chester and made our way to the Racecourse where we found the latest up-to-date farm machinery, such as, bailers, tractors, combined harvesters and the like.

We also found the Food and Drink tent and spent some time in there sampling some different beverages.

That year it had been a very wet season and the Racecourse was renowned for being water - logged, this year was no different.

The two days of preparation meant the tractors and other vehicles had churned the ground into a quagmire and the mud must have been 12 inches deep with a skimming of water on top.

After gorging ourselves in the food tent we decided to have a look around the show ground. We sat on most of the tractors and marvelled at the latest farm implements.

Then we walked towards the cattle stalls and heard someone shout, "Stop him!, Stop him!" The people in front of us were waving their arms and shouting, but then running to one side or the other.

Ray pointed forward, "It's a Bull," he said, and running towards us was a white-faced Hereford Bull, more frightened than wicked, but still moving at a tidy pace. We waved our arms to try and bring him to a halt, but he was having none of it. He passed by Ray at full gallop with a rope trailing behind him. On seeing the rope, Ray grabbed it with both hands and this is when he took off. At first, he took small strides, but still holding on to the rope they got bigger, then bigger still, then giant strides, then falling to the ground he went through the mud like a speed boat, but managed to bring the bull to a stop, after travelling for some distance.

The bystanders duly gave him a well-earned round of applause and he acknowledged his moment of glory.

Bill trying to catch Girt or Elsie

The Cheshire show on one of the dryer years

Bill on a new Ferguson tractor

Bill on a combine harvester

Ray on a fordson major

Nellie's Frothy Coffee Café

By this time, I was fifteen years of age and working full time with Danny on the farm, but beginning to spread my wings at night in Nellie Inchcliffs Frothy Coffee café, near the Red Lion on Chester Road.

One night I was told a lad from Rossmore Gardens was looking to fight me, because I'd been chatting up his girlfriend, but not being aware of doing anything wrong I said "Let him come."

This he did and we met opposite Mrs Profit's shop, by some petrol pumps. We argued for some time, until I lost my temper and threw a left swing connecting with his chin. To my amazement his eyes rolled as he fell backwards to the ground, out cold.

That night, I had my hour of glory. I was the toast of the café, but believe me, it would cost me dearly later.

A couple of nights later Johnny, Ray, and I were walking from Nellie's Café, when to my surprise, a young lady came running up to me shouting "Billy, Billy, how are you?" and threw her arms around me.

As I glanced over her shoulder I could see three rather big, hard looking lads approaching. "Are you Billy Bradley?" one asked. "Yes mate," I replied. "What can I do for you?" Are you the Billy Bradley that laid my mate out?" "Again, I replied, "Yes."

"Then I have come to lay you out," said the larger of the three.

This is when I realised, rather than having any affection for me, the young lady had been pointing me out.

"Where do you want it, here and now, or somewhere private?"

Being somewhat naive, I chose somewhere private. This was in a field up Ledsham Road.

As we walked to the field Ray commented that if the three set about me he would join in and Johnny agreed, but again being naive, we never got the message when the three strangers spent some time and effort lacing up their shoes. We arrived at the field and I stood opposite the lad who had threatened me and put up my hands in a boxing position, only to feel a kick in the groin. At this time, the other two came towards me, but Ray grabbed the larger one and Johnny grabbed the third.

I rushed towards my opponent and got him in a head lock and, whilst swinging him around, I could see Johnny on the ground, getting the kicking of his life.

This is when I realised it wasn't a fair fight and slid down my opponent's legs grabbing his testicles with both hands, then squeezing and believe me, after milking twelve cows twice a day by hand, I could squeeze!!

After listening to his screams for what seemed an age, he shouted "Enough enough." "Are you sure?" I replied, "Yes, yes," came the answer, "Enough." I released my grip and got to my feet to see Ray had faired very well with his opponent but Johnny lay in a heap covered in blood, as his opponent walked away.

All six of us agreed we'd had enough and decided to go back to Nellie's Café to get cleaned up, but on picking Johnny up we could see his face was unrecognisable and he could hardly walk.

Putting his arms over our shoulders, Ray and I carried him back to the café, where we could see the three lads we had just been fighting with. "Come on lets go in and get cleaned up," I said, "No," Ray replied. "Let's get Johnny home."

Not wanting the three lads to think we were frightened to go in I left Ray with Johnny and went in to prove I could, but to my amazement, Nellie shouted, "Out you go, you're a trouble maker and you're barred"!!

The next day Ray and I called to see how Johnny was and were shocked to see the state he was in.

His eyes were swollen and nearly closed. His mouth was purple in colour, he couldn't speak and he was bruised from head to toe.

Mrs Reed, Johnny's mum, who was normally a quiet lady, gave Ray and I the rounds of the table, telling us to stay away from the village and keep out of trouble. We did as we were told for a few days, then I decided I was not being kept out of my own village by people from another town.

So, I decided to go to Mrs Mack's Café at the other end of the Village, but I would still have to pass Nellie's.

I walked up Red Lion Lane and crossed in front of the police station and past Nellie's, but, as I passed, I was jumped on from behind and pushed to the ground and I heard a voice say, "Stand back, he's mine."

The next thing I felt, was a kick to my stomach and one catching me in the right eye, then the words "I'm happy now, leave him there."

I picked myself up and staggered home with an eye that was so black it shone.

Bill outside the Cadet hut in
Childer Thornton with his
black eye

Coming of Age

As I've said earlier, I was spreading my wings and the lads
and I started to go to a dance hall in Eastham
Village called, The Eastbougher.
This was a wooden shed behind a pub, but it had live
bands and plenty of girls, not as we were interested,
other than the fact we could keep each other company
on the long walk home at eleven thirty pm.
The main reason we went, was because we could get a
pint of beer without being asked our age.
Then we started going to the Rifleman's Pub in Childer
Thornton, where we joined the darts team and found
ourselves playing at the Ledsham Hotel at the top of
Ledsham Road. To my surprise, the landlord Mr H, said.
"You had better not win this game Billy, because you'll end
up playing in the Railway Pub, where your Mum works, It
had not occurred to any of us that one landlord spoke to
another.
We are all now sixteen years of age and have spent our
five shillings at the Post Office to buy our provisional
driving licence, which meant if we had L plates on the
vehicle, we could drive a tractor, or ride a motor bike

on the road, or, if we had a competent driver with us, we could drive a car. Now this opened all sorts of ideas, as at that time, the Americans were leaving their Sealand Base and selling off their cars cheaply.

That year, Danny went on holiday to Jersey and left me in charge of the farm with the help of Wilf at weekends and nights after work.

The main job was the milking, but between the milking, I was to land up the rows of potatoes in the middle field.

I did this, using Fashion to pull the scuffle, whilst in the next field, Tom Unsworth was chain-harrowing on his green   Fordson Tractor.

I had never met Tom, but as I rested Fashion, he walked over and asked where Danny was. I told him he was on holiday.

"Has he left you in charge?" He asked.

"Yes," I replied.

"He must trust you then."

"Yes he does," "but I've been on the farm since I was little."

"I believe you're a friend of Raymond, the lad who works for me?"

"Yes I am Mr Unsworth, we're great mates and with that, I said "Must get on, walk on Fashion" as Tom got back onto his tractor and drove off.

Ray was the tractor driver for Tom, which meant he should have started work at eight am, but on many occasions, Danny and I would cheer him on as he jumped over the iron hurdles and ran across the fields at eight thirty, late again.

However, Tom would come to rely very much on Ray,

because when Tom fell ill, Ray took complete control
of the farm and ran it for six months, including the
milking.
Danny returned from holiday and suggested I should take
a week off and go somewhere for a break.
So, I had a word with Bass, who was now working for
Norman Dodd full time, and he suggested we go to
Butlins in Pwllheli, North Wales. We agreed to leave it
to Bass's Mum to book it and we concentrate on
saving money to pay for it.
A few weeks later, Bass came round with the coach tickets
and brochures, saying we leave on Saturday morning.
 We caught the coach at the Red Lion and travelled up
 the coast road to North Wales, which to me was another
 Country.
   However, a couple of hours later, we arrived at Butlins
 Holiday Camp. This was an area covered in
 multicoloured wooden chalets with lots of people
 wearing red coats.
 After booking in, we walked to our allocated chalet,
 which was just down from the main entertainment
 area, but on arriving we found we were sharing with
 two other lads from Stone in Stafford.
 They were good lads, about the same age as Bass and I
 and easy to get on with. We went out to a few places with
 them, but stayed mainly on our own. There were outdoor
 games, indoor dances, skating rinks and lots of girls, but
 unfortunately, most of them were from the Ellesmere
 Port area, which didn't help because the chances were
 they would have known any one of my three sisters.

Nevertheless we enjoyed ourselves and had a good time.
On returning, Danny asked me how I got on with the girls.
Trying to be big, I exaggerated what had happened
between me and a couple of girls and Danny seamed quite
impressed.
But then to my surprise he said, "I hope you used
protection." "What do you mean protection?"
"Well did you use a Durex?"
"A Durex, what's one of those?" I replied.
"It's a thing you wear for protection," then started to
explain how to wear one and where to get them from.
The place he suggested was Walker's Chemist, opposite the
Railway Station and told me they were half-a-crown a
packet.
To prove I had listened to him and to make out I had done
something with a girl, which I hadn't, I decided to go and
buy some.
The problem was, Winny the girl who worked behind the
counter, was a friend of my Mum's and my sister's.
Not to worry, I would wait until she went home and then
ask Mr Walker for a packet of Durex.
It was about five fifteen when I walked up Station Road
saying over and over in my head. "Could I have a packet of
Durex Mr Walker please?" Again and again, I rehearsed it
in my head.
I arrived at the King's Cinema and crossed the road into
the Railway Station waiting room where I kneeled on the
bench seat, looking out of the window across to Walkers
Chemist shop waiting for Winny to go home.
After some time, my knees began to ache, so I turned

June, Crisy, and my sisters, Barb, Jean, ??? Joyce.

around and sat for a moment, looking up at the round clock
on the wall over the ticket office window.
  As it came up to two minutes to six I thought I would run
across to the shop, just before Mr Walker locked up.
  Off I go, clasping a shiny half-crown in my hand, still
chanting. "Could I have a packet of Durex Mr Walker
Please."
  In through the door, I turned left, only to come face to
face with Winny.
"Hello Billy, just in time. What can I get for you?"
  Desperately trying to clear the phrase in my head I said.
  "Could I have a packet of A,As Aspirin please? My Mum's
got a headache" "A large or small one Billy."
My head was spinning, what did she mean a large one

or a small one. "Asprin Billy, large or small and they
come in bottles not packets" she said. "Ere, Ere, large
please" I said stepping forward.

By this time, I was shaking, wondering if she knew what I
had really come in for and once I had handed her the shiny
Half-Crown, I was convinced she did.

I grabbed the Aspirin and my change and bolted through
the door, only to have to go through it all again, the
following day with Mr Walker, but this time he knew what
I wanted and I walked out of the shop like a man. The next
day, I went to work and showed Danny what I had bought
and the only comment he could make was, "Have you any
use for them?" 'No," I replied "I would rather have a
half-crown."

"Yes your better off with this" and passed me a half-crown
and took the Durex from me.

All I can say is although I never got to use the Durex, I
certainly had an experience to remember.

Time to move on

Later that year, Iris a friend of our Joyce, started coming to the farm to see Danny.
"Why is Iris coming to the farm telling me what to do?" I asked Danny. "Well we are getting married and she will be the bosses wife, so she will be telling you what to do."
This sent a shudder down my spine as she had no knowledge of farming whatsoever and I was having none of it.
Later that week, I asked Ray to ask Tom if he would take me on, but Ray came back with the answer Tom wouldn't take labour off a neighbour. I took orders off Iris for a few weeks then met Bass who was now working for Fred Lancaster as a cowman.

"Will you ask Fred if he's taking anyone on."
Bass came back with just the answer I wanted.
Fred would take me on for the summer season.
I gave Danny a week's notice and started with Fred the
following week. I arrived at Fred's yard, near Two Mills on
the Welsh Road and he welcomed me with open arms.
"What's happened between you and Danny?" he asked.
"Oh, he's getting married and she's taking over, so I
thought I'd best leave."
"Never mind, we'll keep you busy for the summer."
Fred then introduced me to Sid, the man I would be
working with in Wallasey, laying a playing field in Walacre
Road.
"You'll be following me on that Fordson Major, have you
driven one before?" he asked.
"No, but I've driven a Fordson Standard."
"That'll do stick on the L plate's and follow me." Sid said
before setting off on a brand-new Fordson Major,
towing a trailer with a set of spike and chain arrows on
board and I followed behind on a very high-wheeled old
Fordson Major.
It had originally been blue in colour but was now scratched
and battered, the rear tyres were tread-bare and the front
wheels had a wobble as you gained speed.
Nonetheless, I followed Sid, as instructed down the high
road through Barnston and on to Wallasey, where I turned
right into Walacre Road.
This took me down a very steep hill, where I could see Sid
in a field full of discarded rubbish, unloading the trailer.
Half way down the hill, I felt the tractor gathering speed,

so I applied the brakes with my right foot but got no response.

I then pulled on the hand brake, still nothing, as the tractor gained momentum.

Realising there was nothing I could do to stop the tractor I concentrated all my efforts on steering it through the gates into the field leaving Sid in a cloud of dust.

Eventually, I managed to bring it to a stop and knocking it out of gear I jumped off saying to Sid.

"Do you know this thing has no brakes?"

"Yes it will be Okay when you have the arrows behind you, just put your clutch in and they will pull you to a stop."

For the next few weeks Fred would drop us off in the morning and pick us up at night in his new Hillman car, along with several cans of T.V.O. fuel for the tractors.

Sid and I, with the help of a couple of other lads, graded, harrowed, rolled, and sowed grass seed and laid the playing field which is still there today. When the job was complete we loaded the tackle onto the trailer hooked it up behind Sid and he set off leaving me to follow behind.

I climbed onto my tractor and headed up the hill, but when reaching the top, found the traffic going across the top of the road was quite busy, knowing the brakes were suspect I stopped by riding the clutch but very soon it began to smoke, so I pushed it down.

Then the tractor started to roll backwards, I knew if I released the clutch it would smash the gears so all I could do was to go back down the hill, but this time backwards.

After wiping my brow and adjusting my trousers, I set off back up the hill, but this time went up the right hand side of the road and took a sharp left pushing in alongside the traffic.

By now Fred had bought a German Combined Harvester, which Sid would be in charge of, getting him the nick name of Heinze with me as a second man. We travelled from farm to farm Combining Wheat, Oats, and Barley until the end of September.

Then Fred bought a Potato harvester and Sid and I went to a large estate farm just outside Chester to harvest a field of potatoes.

On arriving we were met by a young farm manager who showed us the field. Sid lined up the harvester and started to move along the rows of potatoes him on the front driving and me on the back bagging and sorting the potatoes as they came up.

After a few yards the elevators got jammed with potato tops so we had to stop and clear them.

Again we tried, but again she blocked.

Sid then said to the farm manager, who was stood at the end of the row, "it's no good, the tops are too fresh, we'll have to wait for them to die off." The farm manager looked quite upset at Sid's remark and told him the field must be harvested as soon as possible.

"Park the harvester over there and we'll spray them over the weekend." "What will you spray them with?" I asked. "We have chemicals that will kill them off in forty eight hours."

"Forty eight hours, you can't do that, anything that

strong will go into the potatoes." 1 said.

The look he gave me made me think the ground was going to open and swallow me up.

"I can't," he said, "You little know-all, have you been to agricultural college." "No" I replied, "I haven't." "Then leave it to me" Then he turned to Sid and said. "Don't bring that know-all back on Monday!"

By the time we got back Fred knew all about it and called me to one side.

"What's this you've been saying to one of my best customers?"

"I don't think you can spray chemicals onto any plant without it going into the roots, and the root of a potato plant is the potato isn't it?" was my only reply

Sid backed me up by saying at least I was polite when I said it. This is when Fred said "If you can't go back on the potato harvester I'll have to let you go, as it's near the end of the season anyway, but I won't do that until you've found another job."

Of course, some years later spraying crops with chemicals was stopped. That night, I asked Ray if he would ask Tom once again, would he take me on and to my delight he came back with the answer "yes" Tom would. I told Fred, he paid me up, we shook hands and I left on good terms.

I then started with Tom Unsworth or "the boss" as he was known to us all, as second cowman and spare tractor driver to Ray. But Tom was setback somewhat when he found out I had no idea how to use a milking machine. Of course I had only milked by hand.

However, I soon picked it up and between milking I spent

A painting of Studd Farm painted by a local
artist from my memory fifty years on

most of my days bedding down young heifers in loose
boxes where they would spend the winter.
The loose boxes were where the racehorses had been kept
and had stable doors that allowed you to leave the top half
open during the day.
There were about six down the back passage, opposite
the shippons, and four facing the main yard, which was
laid with beautiful stone cobbles. At one end of the
building was a small cottage, which had been for the
groom or stable lad, but was now used for storage.
Across the yard were more stables, which housed the dairy,
our bagging shed where we had our breaks and the garage
which housed the boss's beloved Daimler.

Across the south end of the yard was the farm house, which spread from one side of the yard to the other, and looked into the archway of the north end buildings which led to the airfield, now the site of Vauxhall Motors.

About this time, Bass asked if we could have another go at keeping pigs so I agreed we would go partners in a small litter of porkers. They are bought in at eight weeks old and sold on later for pork.

I remember ordering two bags of pig meal off the corn merchant who came to Toms, not thinking how I would get them home.

Later that week the corn merchant turned up with a load of cattle nuts and two bags of pig meal.

"These two are for you I believe where do you want them?" said the driver. "Little Sutton," I replied.

"Don't go there, I'll leave them here for you to sort out," and dropped them onto the floor.

At the end of that day I said to Ray "I've got two bags of pig meal to get home what do you think^9"

"We'll carry them one each," came the reply.

Now these bags weighed one hundred weight which is 112 lbs.

"Carry them," I said, "over four fields."

"Yes came the answer."

We got them onto our backs and set off down the drive and over the Rivacre Road, over the five bar-gate and on across the big field, over the old golf course and across to the pig pen in the bricky field.

As winter turned to spring we heard the Corporal's Mess at the Aerodrome was holding a dance and members of

the public could buy tickets. This seemed a good idea
as it meant we could have a drink without being
questioned about our age.
The tickets were purchased and in we went straight to
the bar.
"A rum and coke please" I asked the corporal behind the
bar.
"Certainly Sir single or double?"
"Oh, make it a double," I replied.
I downed it in one, looked the corporal in the eye and
said. "Same again please."
The corporal duly obliged and I downed that one.
By this time the other lads I was with had also had a drink
and were heading for the dance floor.
I followed on and asked a young lady.
May I have this dance?
"Dance with you?" she said, "Not likely your drunk."
"Drunk?" I replied, "I'll show you drunk" and made my
way back to the bar. As I ordered another rum and coke I
was joined by Johnny. "What's wrong" he said. "Oh a girl
said I'm drunk so I'm going to show her what a real drunk
looks like."
"I'll join you," he said and ordered another rum.
The two of us continued to drink until I felt cold and
found myself looking up at four feet which seemed to be
standing on the sky.
Then I saw Ray standing next to what I thought was a
policeman, but he had a kind voice as he said. "Come on
lads let's have you up" and clasped my hand to pull me
up leaving me sitting on a three foot high garden wall

with Johnny alongside me.

I looked at Ray and asked what had happened,
"I'll tell you what happened."

"Last night you and Johnny fell over that garden wall and I couldn't move you until the postman came and gave me a hand."

It must have been six in the morning as Ray put my arm round his shoulder and Johnny's arm round the other and carried us staggering from Hooton to Little Sutton.

Left to right Byron, Dave, Bass, Johnny,
Fow, Bill Ray must have been getting
the drinks in again.

The Gloucestershire Runs

In the spring one of the lads said Billy Ellis was selling off
cheap cars and wouldn't it be a good idea to club together
and buy one between us.
This we did and ended up with a four seated car with a
distinct wobble and on checking the cause of the
wobble we found the chassis was held together with the
sidebar of a wooden ladder.
One of the braver lads suggested we take it back to Billy
and get our money back.
After bucking up the courage all the co owners took the
car back, but no money changed hands. We came out
with a soft topped Wolseley Hornet, a car to be proud of.
It was red, with a long sloping bonnet ending with a
chrome topped radiator.
A large chrome headlight mounted on a chrome
pedestal each side. The seats were green leather, two
front, with a bench seat at the rear. The steering wheel
was like a white bone with four thin chrome bars form-

ing the centre of the wheel.

The chrome front bumper was attached to two large mudguards which sloped back to a running board that ran the length of the car.

Not being able to wait to get onto the road we folded back the top and set off for a day out in North Wales.

After visiting several towns and seaside resorts we headed back.

As darkness fell, we noticed other cars had their side lights on so we rightly followed suit.

Then came the headlights these were operated individually with separate switches one for each side.

The left hand side was perfect it shone straight at the kerb or grass verge, but as we later found out the right hand one had a mind of it's own.

On the way down a very steep hill we were dazzled by an oncoming car so to make him turn off his main beam we turned on our right hand side headlight, only to be blinded by a powerful beam.

Not being able to see we pulled up along the grass verge expecting to see a car in front of us but to our surprise we found the chrome headlight had turned completely around on the pedestal and was shining into our eyes, this meant another visit to Bill's.

This time we came out with a very large American Chrysler just like the cars the gangsters used in the films we'd watched in the King's picture house on a Saturday night.

It was black with large front mudguards and a running board each side. It had a large boot lid with an imprint of a wheel where the gangsters would keep their guns, but we only had a spare wheel.

After a few local journeys we decided to go to visit Margaret and her husband on their plum farm in Gloucester. He was affectionately known as Gloucester Bill.

We all clubbed together to fill the enormous tank with petrol and set off around late afternoon, arriving at a very aptly named side road called featherbed lane. We decided we would spend the night there and all curled up on the seats to get some sleep.

The following morning we awoke to the smell of petrol and after an investigation under a very large bonnet we found the main copper petrol pipe had a split about an inch long and every time we started the engine petrol pored out.

As we sat pondering a solution one of the lads noticed the interior upholstery had a piping around it and on further investigation found it was lined with a rubber tube.

This was the answer, cut a two inch gap in the copper pipe and slide the rubber tube on to each end, it worked a treat and we carried on reaching Gloucester Bill's about lunch time.

Bill, Margaret and the two kids were very pleased to see us as they had just started plum picking and took no time in giving us all a box a piece to start picking plums.

Off we went down the field and picked plums for most of that day, returning to the farm cottage, where Margaret fed and watered us very well.

As the evening drew on we all selected a corner of the

barn where we made our bed for the night.

The following morning we were awoke by the sound of Gloucester Bill washing in a water-butt, which had been filled with rain water from the roof of the cottage.

"Morning Bill, why are you washing in cold water?" I asked.

"Because we get our drinking water from a stand pipe half a mile down the lane and we don't waste it by getting washed in it" This made us all realise we must follow suit and get into the water-butt.

We all did just that and made our way into the cottage where Margaret made us a first class breakfast, before loading the car with boxes of plums for us lads and Danny. We said our goodbyes and set off for home.

All went well until the car started to splutter so we pulled over into a lay-by to investigate the problem.

Sure enough it was the petrol pipe, the rubber sleeve had perished and was leaking petrol, so no more ado, we cut another length off the upholstery and slipped it over the copper pipe.

By this time we were getting peckish, but due to the fact we had spent all our money on petrol, meant the only food we had to eat was plums. So away we went tucking into boxes of Victoria plums one after the other.

Very soon we set off again making good progress until one of the lads said he needed to go to the toilet. "Okay we'll pull over and you can go behind the hedge."

First one went, then another, then me, I don't know how they felt, but believe me, my backside was on fire for days after.

The Vulcon Bomber

That year the R.A.F. held an Air Display at Hooton which
was surprising, because sometime before a Meteor Jet
had crashed whilst attempting to crack the sound barrier.
They did this by climbing up into the sky then diving
down to earth but pulling up at the last minute, creating
a loud bang which was known as the sound barrier.
Unfortunately, something went badly wrong on that
occasion as the Pilot never pulled up and went straight into
the ground.
I remember bringing the cows up in the back field a couple
of days before the display, when they started to stampede
back down the field.
Suddenly, the sky went dark, as though it was   going
to thunder and as I looked up, I found myself directly
under a Vulcan Bomber, coming slowly into land on the

runway just the other side of the fence.

He had come in so low he had taken the branches off the tops of the poplars around the swimming baths.

There wasn't a sound as he passed over me and I felt I could reach up and touch the wheels. It was like a space ship going over me.

Then the noise came as he touched down and started his reverse thrust, grass, leaves, twigs were blowing above me as I dropped to the floor.

The heat off the engines was terrific, as I lay flat on the ground, with my hands over my ears before running down the field to calm down the cows and bring them up again.

A Vulcon Bomber as seen in 2015

The following weekend, we decided to go into Chester for a Saturday night out and ended up in a dance hall called the Riverpark, which was the haunt of the American G.I.s, the men that could jive.

I remember walking across the dance floor when the doors burst open and in came the American Military Police.

They were dressed in kahki uniforms with red caps, white gaiters over their black boots and white belts with large truncheons hanging from them. Suddenly they drew their truncheons and started to hit the coloured American Soldiers and threw them into the back of an army wagon. I was told later it was all because a coloured soldier had danced with a white girl, but the girls could see no harm in dancing with a coloured man and continued to do so and some eventually marrying and emigrating to America.

After our experience in Chester, we decided to go to an Irish dance club in Birkenhead, where we tried to do the Irish Jigs, but not with much success, but enjoyed it all the same and continued to go for a couple of months. By this time I would be in my mid seventeen's and expecting to be called up for my two years National Service, unless the boss would sign a deferment paper which would stop me doing it. So, as I knew where I stood, I asked the boss if he intended to sign or not and to my delight he said he would.

This would be around August 1956 and we were bringing up the hay we had bailed on the land each side of the main runway.

The way we did this was to hook up three or four trailers

behind each tractor, wait for a signal from the control tower, then both tractors Ray, on one and me on the other would go full speed down the runway and onto the field.

After all the trailers had been loaded we would hook them up again and wait for the signal from the tower.

At that time the Squadron Leader was James Storrar. Who's tailfin was painted as a barbers pole. His farther was our local Vet and if we had trouble with a cow in the week the boss would ring Chester and Mr Storrar Senior would come out, but if it was a weekend young Jim would come up in his R.A.F. Land Rover and inspect the animal and report back to Jim Senior. On one occasion, but according to Ray it happened to him several times, I remember coming up the runway with three trailers behind me when out of nowhere, six Meteor Jets dive bombed me.

They had come up the Mersey Estuary spotted me on the runway and decided to do a practice attack for some fun. Some fifty years later, I had reason to visit a Vet in Chester and by coincidence it happened to be the Storrar Practice, now being run by James the fifth and I'm glad to say James the sixth is now in waiting.

But back to 1956, this is when our Dougie asked me to go half's with him on buying a German Opal car. It would be his one night and mine on the next.

This worked well for a few nights, until the lads decided, we should go to the Haigh dance hall in Morton on the Wirral.

All went well at the dance, but on the way home, the car began to overheat and steam up.

The first thought was we were out of water, so no more ado, we stopped at a house on the main road and asked if they could oblige us with some water for the car.

"Do you have a container?" asked the Lady of the house.

"I'm afraid not." I replied with a slur in my voice.

"Okay, I'll fill you two milk bottles, that should get you home."

The Lady then disappeared into the house and returned with two quart milk bottles full of water.

"Thank you, do you want the bottles back?" I asked. "No that's Okay keep them in case you need some more water"

We topped the radiator up and started on our way, but found the lights were now fading, so we decided to drive on side lights only.

This worked for a time as there were a few street lights that lit up the road but very soon the radiator started to heat up again, but this time there were no houses in sight.

What to do? Find a ditch, none about!!

I know, we'll all wee in the milk bottles and put it in the radiator. We all queued up to help fill the bottles, but found it very difficult to aim straight in the state we were in.

Nonetheless we managed to pour the contents of the bottles into the radiator and started off again.

As we went on we noticed the lights were going even dimmer and the radiator was getting hotter, but this time the smell made our eyes water, to say nothing about the coughing and spluttering that was going on.

To get home quicker, we took a shortcut down a country

lane, by which time the lights were hardly showing any light at all.

Suddenly out of the darkness came a T junction with an iron hurdle fence straight in front of us.

With no chance of stopping we went straight through the fence dropping eighteen inches into the field.

Scrambling out of the car, we all started to blame each other for the mishap and I believe one or two swear words and phrases were used about the size of my breast and did I have a Father.

But my main concern was, where there any cows in the field and if so, how would we fence them in.

After the confusion had settled down, we started to ponder how we could get the car out of the field.

I know came a voice, "We'll lift it out"

With that, we started to pull the iron hurdles off the car and used the wooden posts as levers to lift the car back up onto the road.

By which time, the battery was so flat the engine wouldn't turn over, so we had to push start the car to enable us to get home, which we did with great care. After a heated discussion with our Dougie about what had happened the car was parked on the grass outside our house and never moved again.

Decision Time

I now started to wonder, if the boss was going to sign the deferment papers.
So one morning, I approached the subject,
"Hello boss I was wondering if you had signed the deferment papers yet?"
"Why are you frightened of going in the army Bill?"
"No boss, I just thought I'd ask."
"Well we'll see how it goes, but don't worry I know two years in the army would kill you."
What the boss didn't realise was, I wasn't working on the farm to stay out of the army, but because I loved it on a farm, "any farm."
This made me think about my position. Should I stay

with the boss, move to a bigger farm, or just do my National Service.

I don't know if the boss was kidding me or just trying to wind me up, but as the weeks went by, he kept mentioning the papers but never got round to signing them.

After many comments about me not being able to take army life I decided to take matters into my own hands. One morning I jumped on the bus to Birkenhead then got the Ferry to Liverpool and made my way up Dale Street to the Army Recruiting Office. There, I came face to face with a rather large gentleman in a very smart uniform.

"Yes lad and what can I do for you today?" he bellowed.

"I've come to join the army Sir."

"Good lad, good choice, but aren't you due to do your National Service?" "No Sir, I work on a farm so I could be deferred, but I think I will join up anyway."

"Well lad how many years do you want to do, three, five, nine, or twenty two."

I thought long and hard, twenty two years, that's longer than I have lived so far, nine?? five maybe.

"I'll go for three for a start sir."

"Right lad, because you've volunteered you can choose the Regiment you want to be in."

"If I sign on today can I have a hat like yours." I asked.

"Yes lad sign here, go home and we'll send you a letter with a travel warrant telling you where to report to."

I signed the papers and left the office, not having a clue about when or where I would be sent or which Regiment I had joined.

Nonetheless I felt a weight had been lifted off my shoulders, as I now knew where I stood.

I went back to work and told the boss what I had done and that I would be leaving the following week.

Having not heard from the army, I started work with Thomas Warrington and Sons digging footings by hand with a group of Irishmen. Good lads each and every one.

The footings were for the council houses that now form Sutton Way, but one Friday afternoon, an argument started between our gang leader and the site Foreman who was a big bully of a man.

Many words went back and forth until our gang leader said.

"If you don't like it we'll all leave."

For a moment the silence was deafening, then all together each man downed tools and walked to the site hut to collect his pay and cards, me included. The rest of that afternoon was spent in the Bull's Head pub in Great Sutton. I say afternoon, but in reality the doors closed locking us in then reopened and closed again at ten   thirty pm

This meant I had to stagger my way home through the Village and down Red lion Lane, where I met Mr and Mrs Briarcliff.

"Hello Billy had a drink have you?"

"Yes Mrs Briarcliff." I said as I tried not to sway to much.

"Well I've been speaking to your mother and she said

you have a brown envelope waiting for you at home which may sober you up."

The following morning I awoke with a blinding headache and hangover but managed to make my way down the concrete stairs into the kitchen where mum said. "There's a letter hear for you" handing me a brown envelope. I opened it with caution and found I had volunteered to be a regular soldier for three years in the Irish Guards.

Now the Brigade of Guards had somewhat of a reputation for discipline, smartness, and a tough training regime. Our Doug who had just finished his two years National Service in

The Royal Engineers couldn't believe what I had done. I'd had the opportunity to be deferred, but instead had volunteered for three years in the Irish Guards.

But still this didn't put me off. "Too late anyway"

Also in the envelope was a travel warrant from Lime St Station Liverpool to Purley Station in Surrey and an instruction to catch a bus to the Guards Depot, Caterham, Surrey.

The good news was that I didn't have to go until early in February 1957 which was a few weeks away.

This gave me the opportunity to earn some good money with J.W.Flather driving a dumper truck, preparing a junction at the end of Rosmore Road for a new road which was to be built, later known as the M53.

As you may have noticed in the mid 1950s Ellesmere Port was booming.

Although Jones's Iron Works, Burmell's steel work's, and the Shropshire Union Canal were slowing down or closing altogether, Council house building was on the rise amid rumours of a car factory being built in the area.

However, the day in February arrived when I had to report for duty, so my sister- in - law Hilda suggested she should escort me from Little Sutton station to Rock Ferry and see me safe onto the train to Lime St Liverpool. After that I would be on my own.

I said thank you and goodbye, as she shook her head, with a very worried look on her face.

The train pulled into Lime St underground and I made my way up to the main Station, where I boarded the steam train bound for London Euston.

I had managed to acquire a window seat and spent most of the time gazing out of the window wondering what lay ahead.

About five hours later, we arrived at Euston Station, where I followed my instructions to go to Waterloo Station and board the train to Purley.

Getting from Euston to Warterloo was a task on it's own, trying to follow the rail line maps on the underground station walls, but I made it.

On arriving at Purley, I made my way out of the station and waited at the bus stop, just outside where I was joined by two other lads, but never spoke. A few minutes later a bus pulled in and to my surprise the bus conductor said "Are you three for the Guards Depot?"
"Yes mate I am, do you know it" I replied, and the other two nodded.

"Yes it's right next to the Lunatic asylum." All went quiet.

A few stops later the bus pulled up and the conductor said.

"This is it lads take your pick which gate you go into, but I know which one I would choose" and pointed towards the hospital.

His comments did nothing for our confidence, as we all walked between the two castellated gate posts.

The Guards Depot Caterham Surrey

For some reason I was first into the Guardroom handing my papers to a very large Coldstream Guard sergeant.

"Name" he bellowed.

"Billy" I replied.

"Billy, Billy what?"

"Billy Bradley sergeant."

"Well Billy Bradley, you've just lost your name because you're late on parade."

Then with a scream that would deafen he shouted "Runner! !"

Out of the back of the guardroom came a khaki flash, it was a lad of my age, but with his arms swinging shoulder high and at a speed, that I would have to run to keep up with.

"Follow that man" the sergeant screamed, "You Bradley, follow that man." I picked up my case and ran after the flash, which by this time had gained a good start on me.

But half way down the tree-lined avenue, I could see up to a dozen squads of soldiers, drilling on the barrack square, with a dozen squad instructors all shouting different orders. This intrigued me so I stopped to watch. Then a giant of a man with a coat-of-arm's on his sleeve, pointed a pace stick at me and shouted.

"That man there, your standing idle boy, get a move on or I'll take your name."

In a matter of minutes and a few hundred yards I had given my name, lost it, and now someone was trying to take it.

By this time the runner, as I now called him had returned, and marched around me whispering "follow me now."

I obeyed his instructions and ended up in what was

called the receiving room. This is where all the intake for that day would be fed, watered, and bedded down for the night.

As night fell, I lay in my allocated bed listening to the other twenty odd lads trying to emphasize how hard they were by naming the hardest parts of their City.

"Hello we-lard, I'm from the Shankhill in Belfast don't you know."

"Hi Jimmy, I'm from the gorbles in Glasgow."

"Well der lad I'm from Scotty Road in Liverpool like."

"Okay boyoh I'm from tiger bay in Cardiff."

I lay there listening to it all but never got involved, because I thought, saying "I'm Billy Bradley from Little Sutton" didn't have the same ring to it.

My Life passed before me

The following day we were told we would all be
going to see our different regimental selection officers,
mine being Captain J.G.F. Head, Irish Guards. I waited
until I was called then entered the office where
Captain Head was sat behind a highly polished wooden
desk.
"Hello William, can you tell me why you want to join the
Irish Guards?"
"Because I like Irish people Sir."
"Very good, do you have Irish blood in you?"
"No Sir, but I worked with Irish lads and enjoy going to
Irish dancing Sir." This was the first time I had been
spoken to like a human being for the last twenty four
hours.
"Well, we have a problem William, the minimum height
for the Guards is five foot nine and you are only just on
the mark, I don't think you will make it. "But I thought I'd

signed on in Liverpool, Sir."

"No, you volunteered to be selected for the Irish Guards and you are now going through the selection process. Unless you can convince me that you can take twenty six weeks physical training, I will have to reject you and send you home."

When hearing this news my heart sank, as I had visions of me having to go home and face the laughter from the boss and others.

Then came the magic words from the Captain.

"You are under-weight, under-height, and undernourished, I don't think we can make a man of you."

"But Sir, you don't have to make a man of me, I'm already a man, because when bigger lads than myself jumped a ditch, I jumped it.

When they climbed a tree, I climbed it, and when they swam the Manchester Ship Canal from the third landing to Manisty Mount to prove they were men,
I swam it too.

That's when I became a man, Sir."

The Officer gave me a satisfying look and said.

"Yes William but could you carry a machine gun on your shoulders?" My reply came back with confidence.

"I've carried a hundred weight of pig food across four fields and over three five-bar gate's to feed my pigs, Sir.

"Oh, you're a farmer are you?"

"No, Sir, I worked on a farm, but the farmer let me keep some pigs of my own."

"If you worked on a farm shouldn't you

have been deferred?" "Yes, Sir, but I've
decided to volunteer." His attitude
softened as he said.

"What hobbies do you have William?"
"I don't have many, Sir, only the army cadets, and I
joined the Star Boxing Club for a few weeks." With this
his face lit up.
"A boxing club, I'll tell you what I'll do, if you will drink
two pints of milk a day and you pass every single test
you are set and you don't lose one ounce of weight in
the next two weeks, you're in."
"Thank you, Sir," I said, about turned and marched out to
join Sergeant McKenzie's Squad"But that's another story"

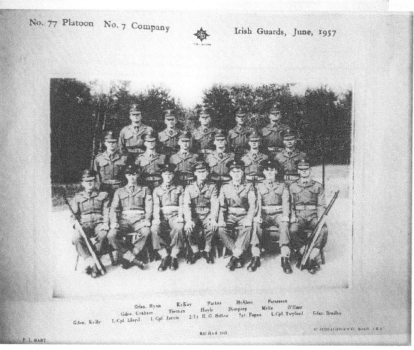

No. 77 Platoon   No. 7 Company   Irish Guards, June, 1957

Gdsn. Ryan   McKay   Parkes   McAleer   Patterson
Gdsn. Graham   Tiernan   Hoyle   Dempsey   Melia   O'Hare
Gdsn. Kelly   L/Cpl. Lloyd   L. Cpl. Jarvis   2.Lt. H. G. Hollow   Sgt. Fagan   L/Cpl. Twyford   Gdsn. Bradley

129

L/cpl Bradley Victoria BKS Windsor   L/sgt Bradley Windsor

L/cpl Bradley Cyprus

Gdsn, Bradley Guards depot
Caterham

Yes that is the same man on the cover

Same milking stool and can 70 years on

Bill sitting on the same stool Danny sat on earlier

After Thoughts

Since writing my story I have had many after thoughts which I think are worth remembering. So here are a few of them.

When the Council bin' men came round they had a horse drawn box trailer which when full, the horse was unhooked and put in front of another empty box, whilst the full one was taken to the rubbish tip on a small wagon that had ramps and a winch to pull the box onto it's chassis, A sight worth watching.

Another sight was the steam driven wagons which carried flour from Frosts Flour Mill's on the Shropshire Union Docks, (now the boat museum) to the Birkenhead Docks for export.

The main part of Ellesmere port ended at York Road, which housed the Open Market and Football Ground and from York Road to Stanny Lane was the Co op horse field which held all there Coal, Milk, and Bread delivery horses.

The Railway Hotel boasted the longest bar in the Northwest and the story goes that Jones's Iron works and Burnell's steel works worked a three shift system, meaning both factories turned out at the same time.

Therefore the bar staff didn't have time to take orders, so the bar was filled with pints and the workers helped themselves to the first pint which was free. Jones's Iron workers, came mainly from Wolverhampton and lived on the Wolverham side of Station Road and were known as Womers, coming from Wolverhampton.

Burnell's Steel workers lived on the Princess Road side of Station Road and were known as Yammers, because of their Staffordshire accent, " Where are yam going." "I'm going wam" " Where are yam going" Translated, is where are you going, I'm going home, where are you going.

Another story to tell is when we camped out on the Rivacre Road next to the big house that had an arched bridge over Rivacre Road onto the old Race course which was now Hooton Airfield. The story is that at the strike of midnight a Headless Woman would ride over the bridge onto the Racecourse. We waited on many occasions, but always found a reason to get back into the tent just before midnight struck.